# WINNERS & LOSERS

# WINNERS & LOSERS

## RANTS, RIFFS & REFLECTIONS ON THE WORLD OF SPORTS

### BOB LATHAM

GREENLEAF
BOOK GROUP PRESS

Published by Greenleaf Book Group Press
Austin, Texas
www.gbgpress.com

Distributed by Greenleaf Book Group LLC

For ordering information or special discounts for bulk purchases, please contact Greenleaf Book Group LLC at PO Box 91869, Austin, TX 78709, 512.891.6100.

Design and composition by Matt Yee
Cover design by Greenleaf Book Group LLC

Publisher's Cataloging-In-Publication Data
(Prepared by The Donohue Group, Inc.)

Latham, Bob, 1959-
  Winners & losers : rants, riffs & reflections on the world of sports / Bob Latham. -- 1st ed.

    p. : ill. ; cm.

  Issued also as an ebook.
  Includes bibliographical references.
  ISBN: 978-1-60832-394-4

    1. Sports--Anecdotes. 2. Sports--Miscellanea. I. Title. II. Title: Winners and losers

GV707 .L28 2012
796                                          2012937396
ISBN 13: 978-1-60832-394-4

TreeNeutral®

Part of the Tree Neutral® program, which offsets the number of trees consumed in the production and printing of this book by taking proactive steps, such as planting trees in direct proportion to the number of trees used: www.treeneutral.com

Printed in the United States of America on acid-free paper

12 13 14 15 16 17   10 9 8 7 6 5 4 3 2 1

First Edition

To my parents: for always encouraging and supporting my forays in the sports world.

And to Kira, who has greatly enriched my sports-related travels.

# Contents

# INTRODUCTION

We have all seen the images. The camera pans to the crowd during a baseball game or a tennis match or right before a basketball player attempts some critical free throws. We see fans with their hands clenched before their faces looking like they are about to go into deep prayer, living or dying on what will happen in the next 15 seconds. Or when something inspirational happens on the field of play, we see complete strangers exalt and celebrate—the billionaire high-fiving the butcher; the guy with the John 3:16 sign hugging the guy wearing a Nietzsche T-shirt.

Well, I'm one of those people (though probably not the John 3:16 guy or the Nietzsche guy). I do not watch sports dispassionately. That's one of the reasons I am uncomfortable in either a press box or VIP section at a stadium, where protocol often dictates that you watch clinically, analytically and non-demonstratively.

When I was 13 years old, for a school project I interviewed Hall of Fame broadcaster Jack Brickhouse—who at the time was the longtime voice of the Chicago Cubs and Chicago Bears, among other notable roles. (The voice you hear making the call on Willie Mays's catch in the 1954 World Series is that of Brickhouse.) I asked the probing question that only a 13-year-old would ask: "Why don't you have glass windows on your booth? Don't you get cold?" Brickhouse smiled at me and responded: "It doesn't matter to me if I get cold. I've got to feel that ballgame. They've offered to put in glass for me, but I always tell them 'no.'" Then once more, for emphasis, he said "I've got to **feel** that ballgame!" His words resonated with me immediately, and have stuck with me since. To "feel the ballgame" is to participate in the experience, not just observe it.

And that is what the essays in this book are about. Since 2006, I have written a column in *SportsTravel* magazine, ranting, riffing and reflecting on what I encounter in the world of sports—the people, the drama, the heroism, the heartbreak, the excitement, the absurdity and the emotion—from Scotland to Siena, Italy, from New Zealand to Uruguay, and from Texas to Chicago.

This book is a compilation of those sports and travel experiences, all written from a fan's perspective, on the places, people and events that caused me to "feel the ballgame," not just see it.

# CHAPTER 1
# PLACES I REMEMBER

# Kiwi Love

*USA vs. Italy, Rugby World Cup 2011*

**December 2011** – Ah, New Zealand, how do I love thee? Let me count the ways.

1. I love that your motto for the Rugby World Cup, which you hosted (and where I spent time in September and October), was "a stadium of 4 million"—and that it was actually true. There is no another country where the DNA of one sport is so ingrained in the culture. And during the RWC, in remote fishing villages or the tiniest hillside vineyards, every single citizen was conversant in the match results from the tournament.

2. I love that your national team, the All Blacks, facing the enormous pressure of a stadium of 4 million people, won the World Cup with a tight, physical 8–7 victory over France. And—due to injuries—you did it with your fourth-string flyhalf, showing the incredible talent you have. That is akin to an NFL team winning the Super Bowl with a fourth-string quarterback. Your citizenry deserved the pride that comes with that crown.

3. I love that your political leaders are true fans like the people they serve. Your Prime Minister, John Key, attended two of the four United States Eagles' pool matches and we were not even playing New Zealand. The fact that your public officials consider themselves part of the throng was evidenced by my encounter with Harry Duynhoven, the mayor of New Plymouth, where the United States played two of its matches. Mayoral status brings with it the title of "Your Worship" in New Zealand. When I addressed Duynhoven as "Your Worship" he stared me in the face and said, "'Harry' would be fine."

4. I love that you were able to overcome tragedy and disaster earlier this year, specifically the earthquake in Christchurch—a city that could no longer host seven of the RWC matches. Many in your country consider the Christchurch area to be the spiritual home of New Zealand rugby, and it is fitting that the All Blacks paraded the championship trophy through the streets of Christchurch (as well as Auckland and Wellington).

5. I love that your national team players are part of your local and national communities, and are known by everyone as simply "Richie" or "Dan" or "Sonny Bill" (yes, the latter is from New Zealand and not from Texas).

6. I love that the people of New Plymouth held a memorial service for the U.S. team on the 10-year anniversary of 9/11 where townspeople spoke from their hearts in their church, and where the reverend revealed that he long had an eagle tattoo on his bicep, to the delight of our Eagles.

7. I love that your 4 million people seemed to follow every team and every player. I traveled with U.S. team captain Todd Clever from New Plymouth to Auckland for a disciplinary proceeding after the U.S. victory over Russia. On the plane back to New Plymouth, the flight attendant came to our seats and said the pilot would like to know if Clever was going to be eligible to play in the Eagles' next match against Australia, New Zealand's archrival. We were as pleased as the pilot as we reported that he was.

8. I love that small towns on the South Island adopted teams from countries such as Georgia and Romania, studied their history and their players, and attended matches in those teams' colors.

9. I love that the president of the New Zealand Rugby Union and former All Blacks great, Bryan Williams, following the awards banquet the night after the final, led an impromptu sing-along with his guitar in the host hotel bar, up to and beyond last call. We could not picture our own Bud Selig doing the same thing in a hotel bar in St. Louis after the Cardinals won Game 7 of the "World" Series.

10. Finally, I love that your spirit is so infectious that it causes reciprocal sportsmanship. In the final—the All Blacks versus "Les Bleus"—only one team would be able to wear their preferred color. The other would have to wear a lighter alternative jersey. French team manager Joe Maso won the coin

toss and the right to select France's color. Remarkably, he deferred to New Zealand, thereby allowing the All Blacks to wear their iconic color, as a show of respect and appreciation for their hosting of the event—a magnanimous gesture. But it was no more that what you deserved.

With (from left to right), Kevin Roberts, New Zealand Prime Minister John Key, Steve Tew and Nigel Melville.

# A Good Walk Unspoiled

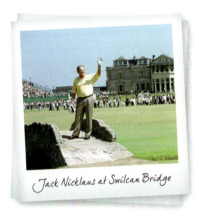

*Jack Nicklaus at Swilcan Bridge*

**July 2009** – It's a Sunday in Scotland and I find myself with a few hours to spare. I am pleasantly surprised that the sun does know where Scotland is after all, and is presenting itself on this day. Thus, it seems to be an ideal time to visit the Old Course at St. Andrews.

Not many sports have a universally acknowledged spiritual center. Wimbledon may have that status in tennis, but you would be hard-pressed to have a consensus as to the signature venue of most sports. In golf, however, there is no course as venerable or as famous as St. Andrews, and a visit there readily confirms its stature. Interestingly, no golf is played on the Old Course on Sundays. Rather, its stewards (the St. Andrews Links Trust) make it available for the public to wander around its legendary features.

I can hear the counterargument brewing: "What about Augusta?" After all, Augusta is the only golf course to host a major every year. But part of the magic of St. Andrews is that it hosts "the Open" (no one in these parts would ever it call it "the British Open") just once every five years, feeding the appetite for it even more. Plus, St. Andrews represents not only the roots of golf but also the present home of golf—the rules of international golf are set by the R&A (The Royal and Ancient Golf Club of St Andrews), right behind the 18th green. Perhaps only Lambeau Field in American football can similarly boast not only a deep connection to the origins of its sport but also current prominence and relevance.

The idea of allowing the great unwashed to descend upon it one day a week serves to perpetuate and enhance the St. Andrews brand, unlike the approach of

Augusta, which is hermetically sealed. The Old Course is of the golf, by the golf and for the golf. So, sorry, Augusta, the nod goes to St. Andrews.

The first thing I note upon arrival in the town of St. Andrews is how accessible the Old Course is from the town itself. Golf courses, and particularly famous ones, are often in remote, set-off areas. In St. Andrews, you can be browsing through any one of countless golf-themed stores in the main section of town and within minutes be walking onto the Old Course.

I stroll up the 17th fairway, perhaps the most famous hole at St. Andrews, and I get close to the Road Hole bunker when a 75-year-old woman walking her dog points to it. "There's where Nakajima needed four shots to get out of," she says, referring to the 1978 Open when Japanese golfer Tommy Nakajima fell out of contention because of his troubles in the bunker. "Same thing happened to Duval," she says, referring to David Duval's travails in 2000. Is everyone in Scotland a golf historian?

I spend some time examining the vastness of Hell Bunker on the 14th hole. I watch as countless tourists have their pictures taken on Swilcan Bridge on the 18th, most in poses suitable for a prom. I wander across the expansive land that forms the 18th and 1st fairways toward the North Sea, where I view another piece of sports history, albeit this one a dramatization: the beach where the training scenes in the movie *Chariots of Fire* were filmed.

Leaving track-and-field and film history behind, I drop into the British Golf Museum before returning to the real-life history that comes alive on the Old Course. And therein lies one of the many beauties of the Old Course: It does not give you the impression that it actively set out to create golf history. Rather, it let golf history create itself upon its ground. I have to think that even the most hardened of professional golfers experiences a different feeling in the years when the Open is played here.

I pop into the Jigger Inn, which is certainly among the best-positioned pubs in the world: an 1850s structure that abuts the Old Course Hotel. I'm pondering the majesty of what I've just seen, as well as admiring the views of the 17th and 18th holes, when a group of 16 golf tourists from the Isle of Jersey—specifically the Royal Jersey Golf Club—walk in, having just finished a round on one of the St. Andrews courses that is open for play on this Sunday. They quickly identify my accent and point to a member of their group, a man perhaps in his early sixties with a healthy head of white hair. "Who from your country does he remind you of?" one of them asks me. Before I can even consider the question, the answer is provided by the other 14, who start chanting: "Jerry! Jerry! Jerry!" Great. Scotland exports the game of golf; we export Jerry Springer. The U.S. trade deficit continues to grow.

*The Jigger Inn overlooking the Old Course*

As I say goodbye to the Channel Islands version of Jerry Springer, the words of Mark Twain are in my head. Golf, he said, is "a good walk spoiled." And it would have been a special, though no doubt frustrating, experience to have walked the Old Course with clubs in hand. On this Sunday, however—not having landed in Hell Bunker, not having shanked a shot into a window of the Old Course Hotel, not having dribbled a ball into the Swilcan Burn, and not having to blast my way out of the "Sands of Nakajima," as the Road Hole bunker became known in 1978—this was a good walk unspoiled.

# A Day at the Races

2010 Belmont Stakes finish

**July 2010** – I had never been to a Triple Crown horse race. But, through some fortunate timing of a business trip and the generosity of a friend, I found myself at New York's Belmont Park in June for the 142nd running of the Belmont Stakes.

There was a time in this country, shortly after the turn of the twentieth century, when the two most popular sports were horse racing and boxing—each accessible to fans across the socioeconomic spectrum. However, it may now be the general impression that championship boxing fights are for Vegas high rollers and the Triple Crown horse races (Kentucky Derby, Preakness Stakes and the Belmont) are for fans as carefully bred as the horses themselves. With that perspective going in, the Belmont provided a number of surprises and revelations.

The first thing I confronted was attire. I was worried that I might have to wear some sort of Bob Baffert/Nick Zito suit to fit in among women with hats the size of Rhode Island. Although there were a couple of Kentucky Derby starter outfits, most of the people were clad as I was—T-shirt and flip-flops—though there were also more than a few looks reminiscent of Rodney Dangerfield in *Easy Money*. Oddly, there were different signs on two restrooms under the grandstand—one for "Women" and one for "Ladies." I'm not sure where the dividing line was, but it may have had something to do with the size of the hat the woman/lady was wearing.

The Belmont has historically struggled to find traditions that would stand the test of time, including this year switching to Jay-Z's "Empire State of Mind" as its theme song. Good luck with that. In 1997, someone invented something called the Belmont Breeze as the signature cocktail of the Belmont, a bourbon-based concoction no doubt meant to mimic the Kentucky Derby's mint julep. This may need some more work in the mixology lab.

I knew going in that the Belmont, by its sheer length (1.5 miles), would show itself as the ultimate test for thoroughbreds. It was also clear why there had not been a Triple Crown winner in 32 years. The distance is imposing. Also imposing is the climate. It is a different matter to run a mile and a quarter in early May in Kentucky than it is to run a mile and a half in the heat and humidity of Greater New York in early June.

In fact, the winners of this year's Kentucky Derby and Preakness chose not to compete in the Belmont, leading to a smaller and more subdued crowd of 45,243.

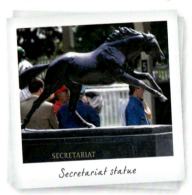
Secretariat statue

In 2002, 120,139 turned out to see if Smarty Jones could capture the Triple Crown.

I also expected to see the legend of Secretariat, the 1973 Triple Crown winner, on display. My seats were almost exactly 31 lengths from the finish line, or roughly where the second-place horse was when Secretariat crossed the finish line in record time. Surely, the Secretariat statue would be as grandiose as the big horse himself. Wrong. The statue looked like something you would see on a wedding cake—a small model of a horse almost invisible to the general public in the paddock area. It's too bad Secretariat's greatness came when New York was having budget problems.

Obviously, any horse, trainer or jockey who wins the grueling race deserves it, so full credit should go to Drosselmyer, a 12–1 shot. But in the absence of a Triple Crown contender, assessing the Belmont's own sporting allure is elusive.

The Kentucky Derby is where we determine the cream of the 3-year-old crop. The Preakness has the advantage of being second, and as long as the Kentucky Derby winner is entered, the buzz of a Triple Crown is still in the air. But the Belmont in a year like this feels like what a day at Belmont Park might have been like 100 years ago.

So the Belmont has sort of a split personality—the center of attention when a Triple Crown is on the line, and the last child in the horse racing family when there is not. In the latter case, perhaps the Belmont should not even try to emulate the Kentucky Derby's traditions. Instead, it should revel in its accessibility for all comers. Take a page from tennis's loud, boisterous U.S. Open, which doesn't try to be the staid, genteel Wimbledon—there is no signature serving at the U.S. Open like Wimbledon's strawberries and cream. Instead it has a little bit of everything. So when someone new to the Belmont asks what the signature drink or the theme song is, the reply could be something that might have come from that most eloquent New York spokesman, Yogi Berra: "We've got nothing. Because we've got everything."

# I'm Going to Jerry World

Cowboys stadium—Arlington, Texas

**January 2010** – There are certainly different approaches to an economic downturn. One approach, obviously, is to tighten the belt and look for ways to contain costs. The other extreme is to go so far over the top that even in challenging times the world will not only pay attention but will pay to take a look at your creation. Consider this second option the *Field of Dreams* option. You take a farm on the verge of bankruptcy and create a baseball field—in the words of Kevin Costner's character, you create something "totally illogical."

Not that there was ever any doubt which option Jerry Jones would choose, but I can confirm that with the new Cowboys Stadium in Arlington, Texas—aka "Jerry World"—he has done the latter. My experience at the first regular-season game at Jerry World, which featured an NFL-record 105,000 fans, confirmed it as simply the biggest, baddest stadium in the country. Jones' $1.2 billion edifice may have established him as both the P.T. Barnum and the Ramses the Great of his time. He sought to build the greatest showplace on earth while at the same time creating a monument to himself in which he may someday request to be entombed.

On this night it was not only the focus of the American football world but also the epicenter of pop culture. My base camp for the game was one of the field-level suites, into each of which Jerry Jones deposited a bottle of Dom Perignon along with a personal note. I did have one question going in: With all the celebrities and riffraff on the sideline, how is it possible to see the field from a field-level suite? Indeed I experienced a wall of celebrity before the game as various Cowboys legends, all of whom would be enshrined in the new ring of honor, strolled by. At one point, I was speaking to the conductor of the Dallas Symphony Orchestra and turned to grab a drink off the ledge, almost elbowing Rudy Giuliani in the process as he took his obligatory lap around Jerry World. Women strolled by in outfits that seemed a little excessive for a football stadium, and few of them bearing their original parts. This was all well and good, but how was I going to see the game once it started?

Dallas Cowboys Rhythm Dancers

The answer lies in the fact that for each of the field-level suites a certain number of seats are allocated in the first level above the field, a quick jump up a flight of stairs that could be accomplished between plays. Having gone up a level to get a better vantage point from those seats, I decided to count the number of seating levels in Jerry World. I realized then that Jones had followed the example set by the fictitious band Spinal Tap: The stadium goes to 11 levels of seating. However, when I tried to take a lap around the stadium to see the various vantage points, I couldn't. Jones had pulled a Titanic as well (and here I was on its maiden voyage!). Various sections of the stadium are segregated, meaning you cannot get in, or even go through, without the appropriate ticket.

Over the field, the giant Jerry Vision video screen alternated between quick replays and 20 seconds of a Dallas Cowboys cheerleader now enlarged to 60 yards long. As the sun went down, I looked toward the end zone doors on the west side and I saw a staggering sight. The architectural design at that end of the stadium features four poles with bird's-nest structures. On them were what the Dallas Cowboys are calling "rhythm dancers," and as they were silhouetted against the western sky it looked like the backdrop of a 1960s variety show.

But there was still something unsettling, something I had not quite been able to process about it, and so I looked again. It then dawned on me what this was. My God, Jerry Jones has built a $1.2 billion stadium complete with pole dancers!

The scenes shown on the video screen during the pregame celebration were also interesting—scenes from outside the stadium so that you could get a sense of the buzz that was going on in the tailgating areas, scenes from the sidelines as Troy Aikman, Emmitt Smith and Michael Irvin chatted together, scenes from NFL games that were wrapping up in other venues. But when an image of Jerry Jones appeared on the screen, 105,000 of his closest friends broke out in appreciative applause for his penchant for excess.

# Renaissance Revival

2008 Il Palio – Siena, Italy

**September 2010** – It's early morning in Florence, Italy. Sure, there are museums and other compelling attractions within walking distance. But a one-hour train ride away in Siena, there is also one of the most distinctive sporting events in the world—one that dates back almost to the Renaissance. As a committed sports tourist, I cannot pass up the opportunity to see it.

It is Il Palio (formally, Palio Di Siena), a horse race around the Piazza del Campo of Siena (the town center) held twice a year, on July 2 and August 16. If you were wondering what that medieval-looking horse race was at the beginning of the James Bond film *Quantum of Solace*, that was Il Palio. In person, it looks and feels more like a scene from *A Knight's Tale*. The setup in the piazza gives the impression that not much has changed since the original "modern" version of Il Palio in 1656. Ten riders ride bareback for three laps on a dirt track around the town center, with people in small grandstands along the side, or hanging out of shops and windows, plus the thousands crowded into the middle inside the track. I was one of the thousands. Each of the 10 riders represents a *contrade*, a city ward of Siena. Each *contrade* has its own colors and mascot, many of them animals.

The day of the race is something to behold as the *contrade* elders lead legions of supporters in their *contrade* colors through the streets of Siena on their way to the piazza. I get caught up in this mass movement shortly after I get to Siena with my 13-year-old daughter, and I suggest that we join a crowd of "giraffe" supporters who are no doubt going our way, as they are led by a guy in medieval attire. Sporting the colors of the giraffe *contrade*, he looks strikingly like Sonny Bono (and I thought Cher wore some wild outfits). My daughter quickly surveys the scene and says, "No, we'll run into turtles" (tortoises actually), and she proves to be right as the giraffes and the tortoises converge on each other like the Jets and the Sharks but with a much more peaceful ending.

This commotion all happens after the more localized "blessing of the horses," in which each of the 10 competition horses walks into the church of the *contrade* it represents to be blessed. You feel a little bit as if you're watching an episode of *Mister Ed* or listening to Shecky Greene performing in the Catskills ("A horse walks into a church . . . ").

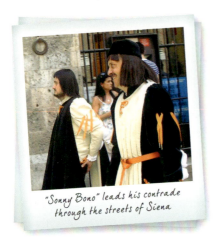

*"Sonny Bono" leads his contrade through the streets of Siena*

We follow Sonny Bono toward the piazza and join a sea of people forming in the center hours before the race starts. The excitement builds amid the pageantry and reaches a fever pitch as the 10 riders enter the piazza. The start is a completely disorganized affair where the starter simply drops a rope when he thinks the horses are reasonably closely aligned. There are no starting gates. The horses take off, and the crowd shouts, screams and cries. On the second turn, one rider slides off the bare back of his horse and into a wall. This, of course, is part of the allure of Il Palio, as the horse is more than welcome to continue the race without his rider.

Indeed, the third lap is even more remarkable as two more riders go down, yet their horses continue and finish third and fourth. It isn't clear whether the riders are felled by their own doing or have help from other riders, but it makes no difference. The race is much more like equine roller derby, and physical contact between the riders, or a rider whipping a competing horse, is not only allowed but expected.

It is a spectacular 90 seconds with the porcupine *contrade* claiming bragging rights until the next Il Palio, and a porcupine supporter to our left breaks down in tears. Never before had I seen anyone cry in the name of a porcupine. The winning jockey,

Luigi Bruschelli, appears to be the calmest man in the piazza as hordes of people storm the track and rip off his porcupine colors. In fact, some fans do not wait for the end of the race to jump onto the track, and the two horses who lost their riders on the last lap smash into perhaps half a dozen overzealous fans who, fortunately, are able to get up before being trampled by the onrushing crowd.

"My God," I say to no one in particular. "Have you ever seen such chaos?" "Yes," comes the answer from my daughter, "in the Milan train station." A fair point perhaps, but Il Palio also brings 350 years of tradition, tear-inducing passion and a town that looks like a movie set—a scene that has no parallel in American sports.

# My Kind of Town

Wrigley Field entrance –
2009 NHL Winter Classic

**February 2009** – Having lauded the 2008 NHL Winter Classic as one of the inspired new events on the North American sports calendar, I decided it was time to put my money where my pen was. Or, more accurately, to put my hand warmers where my Barcalounger was.

Last year, I watched the New Year's Day hockey game between the Buffalo Sabres and the Pittsburgh Penguins—held at Ralph Wilson Stadium in New York—from the comfort and warmth of my living room. When it was announced that this year's game would match the Detroit Red Wings and Chicago Blackhawks at Chicago's Wrigley Field—the shrine of my youth—I could not resist attending in person.

So on New Year's morning, I arose early—a phrase as uncomfortable to write as the act described was to do—to catch a flight to Chicago that would have me at Wrigley Field well in advance of the dropping of the puck at noon. The game-time temperature of 27 degrees, with a wind chill factor of 5 degrees, did not deter 41,000 fans (a significant number of whom had driven from Detroit or were otherwise Red Wings fans) from creating the same neighborhood festival atmosphere that surrounds Chicago Cubs baseball games.

This was the third NHL hockey game to be played outdoors—after one in 2003 in Edmonton and last year's in Buffalo—and the first in a venue dedicated to baseball. Staging a hockey game in a baseball park presented unique challenges. For one thing, the closer to the field a fan is at a baseball game, the better. Not so with outdoor hockey. Those in the lower box seats were forced to stand in order to see over the side boards, which created a reverse domino effect that caused all rows behind them in the box seats up through the grandstand to do the same. Thus, I was on my feet in the third-base grandstand for three straight periods, which accomplished two things: It created an enhanced feeling of excitement, though there was plenty in the park already, and it allowed me to run in place to stay warm without people noticing. While the players clearly reveled in the atmosphere before and after the game, once the puck dropped it was all business. The ice surface was good, and the pace of play seemed faster than last year as the Red Wings prevailed 6–4 in a game that saw 80 shots on goal.

*Hockey at Wrigley Field*

There are several things to take away from the experience: the enthusiasm of the players, the incongruousness of seeing athletes on skates rather than on spikes in a venue so dominated by the latter, the Chicago Cubs and Blackhawks icons that were trotted out and the decades-old cross chants that took place in the stands between archrival Blackhawks and Red Wings fans.

But one thing was uniquely notable: There were no rituals for this event. There was no standard operating procedure, even for Cubs season ticket holders, as to what to do at Wrigley Field on New Year's Day. It was all left to improvisation. Which vending places are less crowded at which times? When do lines to which rest rooms decrease in length? Where are the best seats? It was all virgin territory.

As an example, after the game, rather than retreat to the familiar surroundings of Murphy's Bleachers, I opted for a several-block walk to Cullen's Irish pub for warmth and hot food. And as I pondered the *tabula rasa* on which the live event was created, it occurred to me that the NHL now has a dilemma. There is no question that the New Year's Day tradition of an outdoor NHL game will continue, but it is most likely to continue as a TV tradition where viewers, perhaps overloaded with the cornucopia of college bowl games, can reliably tune in at noon on New Year's Day to see hearty souls braving the elements in an outdoor venue normally reserved for baseball or football. It is, no doubt, a great boost for the NHL on television. But it's a shame when television traditions cannot be turned into live fan traditions as well.

To not have an encore performance at Wrigley Field next year would deny dedicated fans the chance to make the event a New Year's tradition along the lines of the Dallas Cowboys and Detroit Lions hosting National Football League games on Thanksgiving every year. And there is no question that using an iconic venue like Wrigley Field increased both the local and national appeal of the game.

But not to move the event would deprive fans in other NHL cities of the chance to experience the same atmosphere, a national television audience the opportunity to see hockey played in another sporting shrine—Fenway Park and Yankee Stadium seem to be leading contenders for 2010—and two new squads of NHL players the chance to recreate the outdoor pond hockey feeling of their youth. It's fairly certain that the NHL will opt for the latter—which makes me even happier that I made the effort to see this year's event at Wrigley.

# Strawberries... and Heat

Vera Zvonareva

**August 2010** – Wimbledon. The word conjures up multiple images: tradition, grass, the royal box, protocol, players in white, prestige, strawberries and cream. The image that does not come to mind is "heat." During my time at Wimbledon this year, all of the above were on display.

The first thing you notice upon approaching Wimbledon is how close you can get to it without realizing that you are near a world-class sporting event. There are no street hawkers, no pub crawlers, no giant stands or stadiums visible on approach. It retains its feel as a neighborhood club—albeit one with a new retractable roof over its main court that cost more than $100 million. I suppose the fact that Centre Court's name is known the world round may also be a distinguishing feature.

But the grounds are not extensive. Even Henman Hill, which TV coverage is fond of showing as general admission patrons watch the matches on a big screen, is not exactly Woodstock. It's a fairly isolated patch of grass. And on this day, with temperatures well into the eighties, those patrons had an unfamiliar introduction to sweat.

In the surprising weather conditions, the proletariat were allowed to overheat. Royals, apparently, were not. After Serena Williams made quick work of Vera Zvonareva in the women's final, the men's doubles final ensued. Shortly into the match, the roof was closed about one-sixth of the way. Why on earth would they do that, I wondered. I looked at the shadows on the court. It had no effect on the players' ability to see. There was also not a chance that it would rain—rare words to associate with Wimbledon, which installed the new roof in part to address the issue. Finally, my curiosity got the best of me and I asked a nearby usher why the roof had been partially closed. "The sun was hitting the royal box," came the reply. Well, there you go. Somewhere, Donald Trump is plotting his U.S. Open strategy and thinking, "You can do that?"

Centre Court itself is not comparable to any venue in the United States or perhaps anywhere else. First of all, there is the size of it. It is the smallest of tennis's Grand Slam championship courts—seating is only 15,000—and because of its configuration, it is remarkably intimate. The makeup of the spectators is not the usual American sports crowd—there are very few children, and the adults who are there are dressed for church, even on sun-baked days.

Anna Kournikova and Martina Hingis in exhibition match on the now famous Court 18

Then, of course, there is the demeanor of the crowd. No outbursts—only polite applause breaks the regal feel of the place. And no one does anything to rile the sensibilities of the proprietors—perhaps obeying the signs found throughout the bowels of Centre Court. In fact, so much protocol can be daunting. At one point, I was headed back to my Centre Court seat—third in from the aisle. The aisle seat on my row was occupied by a disabled man, while the second seat in on the row in front of me was temporarily unoccupied. So, I thought I would do the considerate thing—I stepped across the person on the aisle in the row in front of me, onto the unoccupied seat, and bounded into my own seat. No harm, no foul, I thought. I was wrong. Handkerchiefs, scarves, and any other manner of wiping cloth were pulled from pockets to dust off any speck of Wimbledon's hallowed turf that I may have deposited on the chair. Looks were directed at me as if I'd just stolen the crown jewels. Or as if I were John McEnroe—a man who had, shall we say, an uneasy relationship with Wimbledon.

While Centre Court is the main attraction, many tennis fans became familiar with Court 18 this year as the site of the longest tennis match in history—the epic Isner–Mahut first-round match that prematurely changed the green grass to a well-worn brown. It is a tiny stage for such a compelling show, similar perhaps to an American college tennis showcase court. How the Wimbledon stewards dealt with crowd control on that court during the three days of the match is not easy to fathom.

And the strawberries and cream? Well, they have actually improved over the years—not necessarily the ideal cuisine to beat the heat, but a staple of Wimbledon to which succumbing seems inevitable.

# The Unsung Funders

Toyota Center, Houston – the bane of "Libertarian Anarchists"

**May 2007** – I've had the conversation before. Sometimes it will start while I'm in a city and I ask for directions to a sports stadium, to which I will then drive my rental car that helped pay for that stadium. Sometimes it will happen when I take a taxi to a sports arena and engage the driver in a conversation about how the new arena is being received by locals. Or sometimes it will arise in discussions with public officials on various sides of the issue of public financing of sports arenas. (I say "arenas" to avoid having to decide on a plural for "stadium"—the stilted but more faithfully Latin "stadia" or the more popular but relative newcomer "stadiums.")

This time, however, the conversation originated in an unusual setting. I was harnessing up a team of dogs in Whistler, British Columbia, to go dog sledding when one of the guides announced that part of our trek would be on the course that would be used for cross-country skiing in the 2010 Olympics. "Oh, I don't want to hear that," said one of the other tourists about to go on the trek. "I'm anti-Olympics. They should take that money and spend it on the homeless." So much for getting away into the wilderness and avoiding political discussion.

My fellow dog sledder would probably have bonded with the local in Pittsburgh who, when I asked for directions to PNC Park, told me that the money spent for the stadium should have been spent to fix potholes, or the self-described "libertarian anarchist" taxi driver in Houston who told me that sports "stadiums" (his choice of words) are monuments to a misguided culture. Look for a lively debate on this issue at the 2008 Libertarian Anarchist convention. Nevertheless, I am able to enjoy my sporting experiences with a relatively clear conscience. Part of the reason is that I, as the traveler, often am the one who is paying for a healthy chunk of the stadium.

It is the tax dollars that I pay on top of rental car charges, hotel bills and the like that often finance sports arenas, not funds that would otherwise be earmarked to combat the homeless problem or pave roads. And, to support my belief that building a sports arena and paving roads are not mutually exclusive, I have generally found the roads around new arenas to be well paved. It also occurs to me that the money that is being, shall we say, "re-allocated" from us sports travelers and put into the local economy has the potential to positively affect the condition of the homeless (how much the homeless problem is related to economic conditions as opposed to other factors is beyond the scope of this column or this columnist).

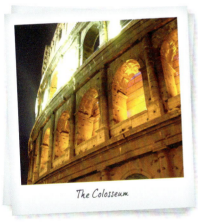

The Colosseum

Sure, locals may also contribute to the financing of sports arenas, through a sales tax increase, for instance, but presumably they and the city they live in will recoup that investment. After all, almost 2,000 years later, Rome is still seeing dividends off the Colosseum. The contemporary landmarks of today can become the historical landmarks of tomorrow. One recent study found that 35 percent of professional sporting venues built since 1990 have been funded in part by tourism taxes.

A case in point is Houston, where the three new sports facilities—Toyota Center, Minute Maid Park and Reliant Stadium—together cost an estimated $1 billion (to the everlasting chagrin of the libertarian anarchist), most of which came from hotel/motel and rental-car taxes.

There was a Monty Python skit in which, during a political debate, one character said: "To boost the British economy, I'd tax all foreigners living abroad." I don't know who was the first to apply this model to the construction of American sports facilities—to tax the tourists so the locals could enjoy—but whenever I hear of somebody objecting to their local tax dollars going to finance a sports stadium,

I remind them that their fellow local citizens are probably already paying for the sports stadia (all right, I went with the stilted plural) in Cleveland, Chicago, Seattle and many other places they travel.

The practice of taxing tourists is not without its critics. The National Business Travel Association says it is a form of "taxation without representation" and a way to bring in added revenue without public officials being accountable to the people who pay it. And others point out that the tourism and event trade may suffer if these taxes reach the tipping point.

So, then, what is an overtaxed tourist to do? Here's my solution: Go see what you paid for. Sure, you may be further contributing to the wealth of a billionaire owner. But when you buy the latest version of Windows, do you worry that Bill Gates may get richer? No, you want to enjoy a better operating system for your computer. Sports arenas do have the potential to make cities—and your enjoyment of a city— better. So if that hotel room is costing you nine more dollars than it might have otherwise, it may be because there is a stadium nearby where you would enjoy food that would represent local tastes, where fans will give you a sense of local culture, and where you will see a star in his or her natural habitat. If you were in Rome, you wouldn't hesitate to go to the Colosseum. So, as long as you're helping to pay the tab anyway, when in Detroit why hesitate to go to Comerica Park?

# CHAPTER 2
# BEING THERE

# Playing With the Players

Steve Buechele

**April 2009** – It's the opening week of the baseball season, and rather than focus on a very unfortunate off-season in the baseball world, I will instead tell one of my favorite baseball stories. Before its demise at the end of the 1993 season, some friends and I held season tickets in the old Arlington Stadium, home of the Texas Rangers. We had a block of tickets in the first row, right next to the visitors' dugout on the third-base side, and the configuration of Arlington Stadium was such that the seats were as close to the infield as you could get anywhere in baseball. Thus, our position relative to both the visitors' dugout and the players on the field meant that we could be a considerable factor in the game, if we so chose.

There is an art to fan involvement in a game. Indeed, one of the rich traditions of baseball is that, thanks to the proximity of fans to ballplayers and the starting and stopping of the game, fans and players can carry on a running dialogue. Unfortunately, some fans don't do justice to this tradition and use foul or abusive language or taunts that are neither in good taste nor in good humor.

We found over the years that most players actually were good sports and enjoyed the repartee once they realized that we stayed on the right side of that invisible line of taste. Seattle Mariners third baseman Jim Pressley (an obvious target) would generally greet us on the first game of a series when the Mariners were in town. Rickey Henderson gave us props in media reports when he became the victim of Nolan Ryan's 5,000th career strikeout after we predicted to him the inning before that it would indeed be him.

Sometimes, however, the payoff is delayed. One of my ticket partners (we'll call him Scott) had a unique approach to communication with third basemen. Usually our comments were reserved for opposing players, but Scott targeted the Texas Rangers'

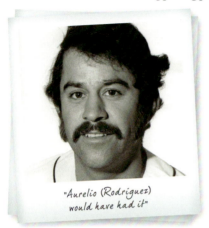

"Aurelio (Rodriguez) would have had it"

own third baseman, Steve Buechele, who played for the team from 1985 to 1991. Scott had a particular fixation on Aurelio Rodriguez, a journeyman third baseman whom Scott had seen play for the Washington Senators in one of their last years before they, like Scott, moved to Texas. So while we were busy getting into the heads of opposing third basemen, Scott would say things to Buechele like, "Steve, I want you to play like Aurelio this year." "Steve, you're looking like Aurelio." "Steve, Aurelio would have had that one."

This would go on every game we attended, but Buechele never gave any indication that he was paying attention to these bizarre utterances. Then, one day, in his last season with the Rangers, a lazy ground ball came bounding into foul territory. Buechele backhanded it, close to our seats, and was about to turn and throw it back to the pitcher, when his eyes betrayed a quick moment of decision. Buechele took a step toward the pitcher, but instead threw the ball backhanded into the chest of Scott, sitting in the front row, and said to him: "Aurelio would have had it."

Several years later, I was in Chicago with some fellow Stanford alumni to catch a late season Cubs game at Wrigley Field before heading to South Bend for a Stanford–Notre Dame football game. By this point, Buechele had been traded to the Cubs, though he was injured and not in the lineup for this game. Buechele was also a Stanford alum, and he knew some people in our group. To my surprise, he showed up at Murphy's Bleachers just outside of Wrigley Field after the game to reunite with some of his classmates. A mutual friend introduced us, and I told him of my appreciation for his play during his six years in Texas from the closest seat in the house to his position. I revealed my favorite memory of him in a Rangers uniform—the time when he good-naturedly (albeit justifiably) bounced a ball off of Scott's chest. "That guy was in your ticket group?!" bellowed Buechele. By this point, others had picked up the gist of the story and started asking, "Wait, Steve, what did you do to the guy?"

The tale then told from Buechele's own lips was even better than the one I had been telling since the incident. "OK, I'm playing for the Texas Rangers for six years," he began. "The entire time, I hear this guy yelling in this whiney voice saying 'Aurelio would have had it. Hey Steve, play like Aurelio.' Anytime I heard this, I would ask the third base umpire, 'What does the guy look like?' I didn't want to look at the guy and acknowledge him myself. The third base umpire would describe the guy: 'Middle-aged, short dark hair, big ears, self-satisfied grin on his face.' So it's my last season there, and a ball bounces into foul territory, and I get ready to throw it back to the pitcher. Out of the corner of my eye I see a guy who fits the description that every American League third base umpire had given me over the years. So I take the ball and go 'boom'—right into the guy's chest. I look at him and say: 'Aurelio would have had it.'"

As laughter ensued among the group listening to this story, Buechele put his arm on my shoulder, and quietly whispered into my ear, "Did I get the right guy?"

# Deconstructing Le Tour

Tour de France

**July 2008** – It's July, and of the various offerings the sports world dishes up this month, the one that is sometimes mysterious to the American sports audience is the Tour de France. Those Americans who are lucky enough to be in France at the time of the race often ask two questions: "How do I watch the Tour de France?" and the more philosophical "Why should I?"

Let me preface this by saying that I am not a cycling guy. Therefore, I approach the Tour de France the way a general sports fan approaches the race. But I have been lucky enough to see several Tours in the past five years from different vantage points and can offer my amateur perspective.

By far, the greatest viewing experience at the Tour de France is to see a mountain stage. And if you pick one of the legendary mountain stages, there is nothing like it in professional sports. Alpe d'Huez, where the Tour has a stage every three years or so, is the ultimate in this category. On the 14-kilometer road up the mountain there may be as many as 700,000 people lined up five deep the entire way up. Think "Barack Obama campaign rally" for nine straight miles. The course is full of hairpin turns and is a brutal climb, so the pace is slow enough to be able to focus on particular riders, and it is at the end of a long day during which the competitors have already gone up and down other mountains. You can see suffering in their faces, you can see their character being tested, and you can appreciate what they have done from a distance of only a few feet away as they go by. And mountain stages offer one monstrous party—ignited by those who have staked their claim to their viewing perch many days in advance.

At some point in your life, it is worth watching the Tour pass through a small town. To me, the essence of the Tour is its ability to be both the marquee event of its sport and remarkably accessible. You can sit in a pub in the middle of a small French village and watch on TV so you have an idea of when the riders will be coming. When the lead rider is about half an hour away, you walk down the street or to the outskirts of town with several hundred people. The parade cars go by first, and then 190 of the greatest endurance athletes in the world come pedaling through your town.

2003 Tour de France passing through Saint-Jeoire

You can't believe how fast they are going, especially when it looked so effortless on television. You can't believe how closely packed together they are, and how much they rely on no one doing anything stupid. The downside of watching the Tour de France like this is that unless there is a breakaway from the peloton, on these flat stages the whole pack goes by in about 20 seconds.

Watching the Tour de France at the end point of a stage is another option. Most stages finish in a moderately sized and hospitable town where a grandstand will be set up for viewing the race. There are several advantages to this scenario. First, you get to see the riders actually racing at the end. Second, you gain an appreciation for the operational details that go into organizing this event. It's like the circus moving to a new town every day—broadcast trucks, team trucks, sponsor trucks, souvenir trucks, grandstands, restraining fences, etc. And you see a podium ceremony with all of its rituals.

If you want to see as many riders individually as you possibly can, a time-trial stage may be the ideal solution for you. You're guaranteed a close-up view of each rider because they go by on their own, having started three minutes apart. This provides something to watch over a much longer period of time—hours as opposed to minutes. The downside, of course, is that you only get to see the riders race against the clock and not against each other.

The image of the Tour de France that many Americans have is Paris on the final day when riders do multiple laps around the Champs Élysées. This is the only place where you get to see them go by more than once. Of course the race is usually decided by this point and the stage is largely ceremonial.

The upside to being in Paris is that the final podium ceremony is special. The setting in the middle of the Champs Élysées with the Arc de Triomphe in the background provides one of the great backdrops in sport. Surprisingly, despite the number of fans watching the final stage, Paris is not the mess you'd think it would be on this day. It's possible to go perhaps a mile from the finish line and have a relatively quiet dinner outdoors.

To move from the practical to the metaphysical, why watch the Tour de France? What these guys do on a daily basis over a period of more than three weeks is absolutely superhuman. It doesn't take long before you appreciate the level of endurance, the tactics and strategy, the teamwork, the courage and even a pleasant degree of nationalism.

# My NASCAR Experience

*Ready to ride after signing my release*

August 2008 – Having been born north of the Mason-Dixon Line, I never had any particular affinity for or connection to NASCAR racing. If I thought of auto racing at all, it was Formula One, Indy Car and NASCAR, in that order—except for perhaps Memorial Day weekend, when Indy Car racing would take the top spot. Thus, finding myself recently at a NASCAR track, and in an actual NASCAR Sprint Cup race car, was about as unlikely as Michael Vick walking into the Westminster Dog Show.

If I had any fondness whatsoever for NASCAR, it was as a result of being amused by the differences in the parlance of the various versions of auto racing. Whereas a crash in Formula One would be described as "an incident," the NASCAR description would be something along the lines of, "Well, a couple of the boys got together in Turn 3."

Nevertheless, in one of the more robust corporate outings I've been invited to in a while, I had the opportunity to participate in the Team Texas NASCAR experience at Texas Motor Speedway—meaning that I was able to take four laps in the passenger seat of the Team Texas Jack Daniel's 07 car.

Not only was it an exhilarating experience, but I have newfound appreciation for what the good ol' boys in stock cars do on Sundays.

The first thing that you notice is how soberly the driver and the team approach and prepare even for practice laps. The cars themselves are groomed as if they were race horses, with every detail being reviewed by the team before and after each practice run.

If you think you are out for a joy ride, the attitude of those in whom you put your trust makes you realize that there is still something inherently dangerous about driving a car at 170 mph. The team members and driver clearly have great faith in each other.

Thus, when you hear a driver on any given Sunday talk about how "we" finished, that is not lip service. There is very much a team behind the wheel of that car.

The feeling that this is not something to take lightly is reinforced by the flame-retardant race suit as well as the thick helmet that you are required to don, not to mention the monstrous release of liability that you must sign before crawling through the window into the passenger seat of the car. Once you're there, the team fastens your racing seat belts so tightly that movement is not an option.

"My" car on the track

Then there is the sound. While you can appreciate the sound of the engine from the stands, hearing it so close to your seat makes you feel like you are inside the sound itself.

There are five cars on the track, and I am in the lead car. After being catapulted out onto the track, you wonder what that first turn will feel like. Since the hallmark of NASCAR is that you are in a stock car, the view from the passenger's seat is not uncommon. What is uncommon is to be heading toward a wall at 170 mph and not slowing down.

As the centrifugal force starts exerting itself, you wonder why the back end of your car is not flying into the wall. Then, astoundingly, you look to your right and there is another car about two feet away. Your concern about the wall is replaced by admiration for the driver's ability to hold such a true line, despite the speed and forces at work, that there seems to be no danger that the "boys will get together in Turn 3."

You come to realize that Texas Motor Speedway has only one true straightaway. While it appears on the grandstand side of the track to be a relatively straight passage, in reality you are making one long, gradual turn that can be felt keenly by driver and passenger alike. Again, you appreciate what it takes to make it just one lap around the track safely with four other cars in close formation. That appreciation does not wane, nor does the bewilderment wear off, over the next three laps.

Stepping out of the car is a bittersweet moment. While the phone call to your lawyer to tell him that he can now put your will back into the safe is a pleasant one, the truth is that you want to get right back into the car and do the whole thing all over again.

Not being able to do so, you extrapolate from your experience. Four laps alone seem to be a draining experience requiring considerable skill and effort by the driver. Imagine doing that 30 mph faster for several hours, not with five cars driving cooperatively but with 40 cars all racing against each other. And imagine that you have to keep that flame-retardant suit on for a few more hours on a hot afternoon in a car that is not exactly equipped with air conditioning (or a good sound system, for that matter).

Versions of the NASCAR experience, including the Richard Petty Driving Experience, which the racing legend started in 1994, are available at more than 20 racetracks across the country. Believe me, it's an effective antidote to any auto-racing snobbery.

# Too Much to Ask?

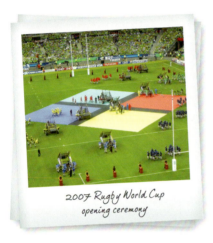

2007 Rugby World Cup opening ceremony

**December 2007** – The holidays are rapidly approaching, and that gives me a moment to look back on the year, while also looking ahead at my hopes for the future. This fall, I spent much of my time in France for the seven-week Rugby World Cup, the third-largest sporting event in the world. Anecdotes from that experience are still on my mind and thus help to illustrate my holiday wish list.

I wish that sportsmanship and respect for your opponent weren't antiquated notions. In that regard, I wish that all youth sports teams throughout the world had seen these traits exhibited at the Rugby World Cup in Lyon, France. There, top-ranked New Zealand played the lowest-ranked team in the tournament, Portugal. After an overwhelming victory by New Zealand, players from both teams stayed on the pitch to kick a soccer ball around—New Zealand's world-famous rugby stars playing pick-up soccer against the Portugal unknowns; it was quite a sight.

I wish that all sports in the world had the ethos of rugby, a sport in which the eventual world champions, South Africa—after eliminating Fiji from the tournament—remained on the field for some 15 minutes while Fiji saluted and then entertained the crowd with a Fijian war chant, so that the two teams could leave the field together.

I wish that government officials in this country weren't held to impossible standards and could act like regular human beings—like the French Cabinet minister, who at a banquet during the World Cup stated that one of the best things about having her job was her ability to visit the teams in the locker rooms. And she was not shy about expressing her observations and desires while there! If you were to make those very entertaining comments in this country, you would soon be looking for a new job.

I wish that I could see more breakout moments for an up-and-coming athlete in any sport. Such a moment happened in Stade de la Mosson in Montpellier when an inspired and courageous U.S. team played against the eventual champions, South Africa. U.S. wing Takudzwa Ngwenya left World Player of the Year Bryan Habana in the dust to finish off an amazing try (rugby's equivalent of a touchdown). It was Ngwenya's first international tournament and he beat Habana, who is generally regarded as the fastest man in rugby, on a try that spanned 95 meters. The play was later recognized as the "world rugby try of the year."

In a related wish, I wish that more world-class athletes had the graciousness of that same Bryan Habana when he commented, both privately and publicly, on that moment of glory for the United States.

I wish that more world-class sporting events were staged in towns the size of Montpellier, Toulouse, Bordeaux and Lens, where virtually the whole town attends the events and then spills out into the streets or town center afterwards to create a true sporting festival.

I wish that more hosts had the dexterity of the French Rugby Federation, which hosted a World Cup final that featured three heads of state (France, the U.K. and South Africa) and at least three princes (William and Harry of England, Albert of Monaco), and then, two hours later, staged an end-of-tournament party that opened with a performance by "Monsieur le Sock," a man who performs wearing only . . . well . . . a sock. Now that's range!

I wish that France would always be as festive and welcoming as it was during the World Cup. And, while we're at it, can they keep that giant rugby ball in the middle of the Eiffel Tower? (It's the only time that anybody can remember the French allowing anything to hang in the middle of the Eiffel Tower.)

I wish that there were more times when a country—any country—was totally focused on a sporting event that isn't historically its national sport. In Argentina, the soccer match between Boca and River Plate in October had its starting time adjusted in order for the nation to watch Argentina play for a spot in the Rugby World Cup semifinals.

I wish that disciplinary proceedings that affect an athlete's eligibility would inspire confidence. I represented Paul Emerick, one of the best U.S. players, before a disciplinary board in Paris after he was cited for a dangerous tackle. He fell victim to an inconsistent and selective disciplinary system. So I'm wishing that Paul gets a chance to play in a full complement of matches in the 2011 Rugby World Cup in New Zealand.

The Eiffel Tower during the Rugby World Cup

I wish that we had moments of singing the United States' national anthem that could compare with 70,000 Frenchmen singing "La Marseillaise" or 60,000 Englishmen singing "God Save the Queen" in a full stadium. Perhaps it is because "The Star Spangled Banner" is so hard to sing. Or perhaps we dilute its impact by playing it at every local sporting event rather than saving it for truly national or international events. Whatever the reason, we don't belt it out the way an anthem should be belted out. Instead, we save our group-sing passion for rock anthems like "Stairway to Heaven" rather than our national anthem. I wish that could be reversed.

I wish that volunteerism in sports would continue to shine and even inspire volunteering outside of sports. There were more than 6,000 volunteers helping to put on the World Cup in France, and they really made the event possible.

Mostly, I wish I didn't have to wait four more years to enjoy the ultimate gathering of the world rugby family as it reminds me of what I love about sports.

# Seven-Day Adventurists

2011 NFC Championship Game at Soldier Field

**April 2011** – It was 7:25 a.m., January 23, when I boarded a plane in Dallas bound for Chicago. Seven days earlier, the Chicago Bears had defeated the Seattle Seahawks in a divisional playoff game to secure home field advantage for the NFC championship game, an unexpected achievement for an inconsistent team. The Bears' victory was made even sweeter for me by a phone call that came shortly after the end of the game from my longest-tenured friend in Chicago, a Bears season ticket holder, who told me he had a ticket for the game with my name on it.

This would be the first time the Bears and their archrival Green Bay Packers had met in the postseason since 1941. If you were not raised in Chicago or Green Bay it is hard to describe what the word "Packers" means to a Bears fan and what the word "Bears" means to a Packers fan—whatever it is, it's not love. "You can either come now or wait until 2081 when it happens again," deadpanned my friend.

I had an additional incentive to make the trip. I wanted to be part of the de-wussification of America. Several weeks earlier Governor Ed Rendell of Pennsylvania had cited the cancellation of an NFL game in Philadelphia due to anticipated weather conditions as evidence that we have become a "nation of wussies." Thus, if there was going to be an NFC championship game of such consequence, played on the shores of Lake Michigan, in 15-degree weather at kickoff with the temperature dropping throughout the game, I wanted to do my part to get Rendell's America back on track.

My early Sunday morning flight the day of the championship game provided some interesting insight. I encountered a dozen people in the boarding area or on the plane doing the exact same thing I was—by my count, 11 Bears fans and one Packers fan, well-bundled with all manner of cold-weather accessories in their day packs. Call us the Down Dozen. As I took my seat, I realized why this impromptu group of non-wussie sports pilgrims was assembled on this particular morning: the seven-day advance purchase policy of most airlines.

The overachieving Bears were no certainty to make the conference championship game, so no one without a general wish to be in Chicago in late January would have planned a weekend trip well in advance. It was not until the clinching victory over the Seahawks, seven days before, that we diehard Chicago transplants, scattered around the country, reacted quickly to see a once-in-a-lifetime event.

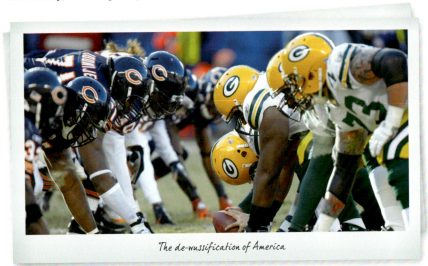

The de-wussification of America

As I made the two-hour flight to Chicago in the only warmth I would enjoy all day, and having spent the previous two months engaged in debate over the merits of a major college football playoff system, I realized one of the challenges such a playoff would present. If there were college playoffs, as a fan of a team that is progressing from week to week, which game do you go to? When do you reserve your airline tickets? How can you make a weekend of it in the location where the game is played when you don't know until seven days before that your team will actually be in a game?

One reason the NCAA basketball tournament is so phenomenally successful is because it is able to get around this problem. There are eight teams per venue, meaning that even though the games are held at a neutral site, the event depends less on the fan base of any one participating team. Even then, for traveling fans who are tethered to a participating team, if your team wins the first game, it plays a second time on the same weekend, thereby creating a greater incentive to make the trip. Additionally, the tournament is split up regionally to cut down, somewhat, on travel. The arenas are, at least for the early games, less than one-third the size of most stadiums where NCAA football playoff games would be played.

Nevertheless, it would be nice to see an evolution of airline ticketing policies that would make it easier for sports fans to spontaneously follow, physically, their teams (yes, I know, frequent-flyer miles can always be cashed in). As the debate continues over an NCAA college football playoff, perhaps someone needs to bring some forward-thinking airline officials into the discussions. Having said that, the fact that the seven-day advance purchase policy caused each of my new friends among the Down Dozen to be on the same itinerary in January added great spirit to the Sunday flights—the outbound segment being somewhat more joyous for a Bears fan than the flight back.

# Respecting the Davis Cup

The Davis Cup — recognize it? Probably not.

**September 2011** – Whereas golf's Ryder Cup is a much anticipated event on the sporting calendar every two years, its tennis cousin, the Davis Cup, exists somewhat incognito in the United States. Part of the reason may be that the annual competition takes nine months to complete rather than a single weekend, challenging the already challenged attention span of us Americans. Sixteen nations in the "World Group" play a knockout competition, with the round of 16 in March, the quarterfinals the week after Wimbledon in July, the semifinals the week after the U.S. Open in September, and the final in early December. But the location of each "tie" (the Davis Cup word for head-to-head competition that consists of two singles "rubbers" on Friday, doubles on Saturday and two more singles rubbers on Sunday) is not known until a few months before the match, unlike the Ryder Cup, which is determined years in advance. The choice of venue (and playing surface) goes, generally, to the nation that did not host the last head-to-head match between the two countries.

Add to this little-understood format the fact that many top players make themselves unavailable for Davis Cup play, which may be partially understandable since the quarterfinals and semifinals take place so close to the two leading tennis majors, and you can see why the event may not be embraced by general sports fans. The present U.S. team, however, of Andy Roddick, Mardy Fish and the doubles team of Bob and Mike Bryan deserves better. These guys have dedicated themselves to Davis Cup play (Roddick is second only to John McEnroe in Davis Cup singles wins by an American) and are worthy of our support. So support them I did, by attending the quarterfinal tie against Spain—winners of two of the last three Davis Cups—in Austin, Texas (Roddick's home town), in July. And I can unequivocally state that if you ever have a chance to see a Davis Cup tie in the United States, do it—especially since ties are often played in places where there is no ATP Tour stop.

The atmosphere in the sold-out Frank Irwin Center was fantastic—as passionate and loud as anyone can remember an American Davis Cup crowd being. And that's one of the beauties of Davis Cup play: Fans get to be boisterous and partisan and step out of the staid behavior that characterizes many a tennis competition. The introductions at the beginning of each of the three days of competition are NBA-style, an analogy that Jim Courier, the new U.S. Davis Cup captain, furthered a bit by abandoning tradition and wearing a suit rather than a team uniform. During changeovers there were various forms of entertainment, including a band. So what does a partisan band play at a tennis match? Well, while the Bryans were up 5–4, about to serve for the third set in the doubles match, the band broke into "25 or 6 to 4" by Chicago. Nice touch.

Fish played two grueling, pressure-packed singles matches, losing 8–6 in the fifth set to Feliciano Lopez on Friday, and in a four-hour, four-set thriller on Sunday to Spain's David Ferrer, who, after his performance in Austin, should also be elevated on tennis's pedestal. But the must-see guys are the Bryan twins, who kept the United States alive on Saturday by winning their 18th Davis Cup doubles match (against only two losses). These guys and the Davis Cup are a perfect match. After the United States lost both singles rubbers on Friday—Roddick losing to Ferrer— the Bryans turned the whole mood of the weekend around. Their enthusiasm is infectious. Constantly moving, bouncing, bobbing and weaving, they pulled off one of their great brotherly chest bumps after one of the greatest doubles points you will ever see, in the fourth set. These guys have an Olympic medal (2008), a Davis Cup championship (2007) and 11 Grand Slam doubles titles, yet shockingly they may rank below the Winklevoss twins in pop-culture recognition. That's a shame. The only category where the Winklevosses are ahead of the Bryans is in lawsuits against Mark Zuckerberg.

Aside from the disappointing loss to Spain in this tie, there was little wrong with the competition or the way the U.S. team represented itself. And with Spain and Serbia each in the semifinals, there is the tantalizing possibility that this year's Davis Cup could be decided in December by a match between the top two players in the world, Novak Djokovic and Rafael Nadal. That could indeed put the Davis Cup back on the sports radar, where it rightly belongs.

*2011 Davis Cup — Andy Roddick vs. David Ferrer*

# Chunnel Surfing

Henley Regatta

**January 2008** – At a recent holiday gathering, I was asked by the college-aged son of a friend what I would recommend that he do in Europe after concluding a junior-year-abroad program in the United Kingdom.

I started to offer insights on the standard trip through Europe with obligatory stops at historical sites and music festivals until an idea came to me. It struck me that this guy had a chance to do something in one summer—even on a backpacker's budget—that took me three decades to do. My advice was to take advantage of this opportunity and see the full smorgasbord of legendary sporting activities that take place in early summer around the United Kingdom and France.

There will always be time to see Stonehenge or the Chartres Cathedral. They are there to see 365 days a year. So, my advice—which you can use for yourself or for an equally eager college kid—is this: Become a sports tourist. It's not too early to start your planning now.

Let's assume you are freed from your vigorous study regimen, or your job as the case may be, by Memorial Day weekend. I suggest that you start your sports-travel adventure in Monaco. If you're on a budget, you will probably not be staying in Monaco; you'll be staying in more affordable villages in France, perhaps 20 minutes away.

The Monaco Grand Prix, the granddaddy of the Formula One Circuit, takes place on May 25. You can get there several days beforehand, find an outdoor watering hole by the harbor, and watch the Formula One teams arrive in town. It is a spectacular atmosphere. On race day, get in touch with your inner Leonardo DiCaprio by attempting to penetrate the glitterati despite traveling around as a backpacking student.

From Monaco, work your way up to Paris for the French Open, May 25 to June 8. The French Open at Roland Garros is by far the best experience for a spectator of the four Grand Slam tennis tournaments. The food is good, the weather is generally cooperative, the matches last longer because they are on clay and the access from virtually anywhere in Paris is relatively easy.

Monday, June 2, would be the optimal day to be there since you will be able to see most of the seeded players. And hey, you're a sports traveler, so let everyone else go back to work that day and you can enjoy a full day at Roland Garros in peace. In fact, while you're at it, stay there for the week.

On June 11, the first practices for the 24 Hours of Le Mans will be held. Get into town, find yourself a spot at the primary campground used for the race, and catch up on your sleep before the 24-hour race starts on June 14.

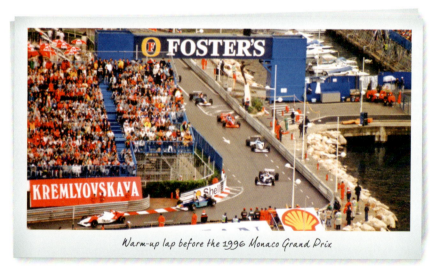
*Warm-up lap before the 1996 Monaco Grand Prix*

It will then be time to work your way through the Chunnel or over land and sea if you prefer (and your budget may require you to prefer) to England. Either way, make sure to arrive by the start of Wimbledon on June 23.

Even though the French Open is the most enjoyable tennis Grand Slam event to attend, Wimbledon does need to be experienced and seen at least once. It is a little bit easier to deal with during its first week, before the really large crowds pile in for week two. The tournament runs from June 23 to July 6.

Seize the opportunity to see some reasonably well-known players on the outer courts. And don't worry about seeing the last four days of Wimbledon. Trust me, you will have seen plenty of tennis by this point in your journey.

Instead, head a short distance west from London and catch the Henley Royal Regatta on the River Thames, July 2 to 6. The first regatta was staged in Henley in 1839 and the lively and festive event has grown each year.

Now it is time to start making your way back to France in order to arrive in time for the start of the 95th annual Tour de France, which lasts for almost the entire month, running from July 5 to 26.

The tour's start coincides with Wimbledon's last week and the weekend of the Henley Royal Regatta. Thus, if you hurry, you could head back across the English Channel in time to catch the tour's start in Brittany. The mountain stages are always exciting to watch and this year the tour even enters into Italy for two days.

After that, work your way back to England for the British Open at Royal Birkdale, July 17 to 20. The British Open is sometimes a challenging tournament to see—both because of where it is sometimes held and the often less than pleasant weather. You are lucky this year: Royal Birkdale in Liverpool is fairly accessible compared to other courses. So, seize the opportunity and enjoy some serious links golf.

Despite my initial comments on this column advocating a sports feast this summer rather than a music festival, there is a certain musical heritage in Liverpool that you might want to . . . nah. Stick to sports this time around. It's an opportunity you may never have again. Just ask your parents.

# The Other All-Star Game

2007 NHL All-Star Game

**March 2007** – Like a high school class that had not had a homecoming game for three years, the stars of the NHL, past and present, gathered in Dallas on January 24 for the renewal of the NHL All-Star Game. With the 2005 game cancelled because of NHL labor strife and no game last year due to the Winter Olympics, the players seemed genuinely enthused and anxious to showcase their sport.

The all-star game this year was changed to a midweek affair with a salute to NHL legends on Monday night, a Young Stars and Skills competition on Tuesday night, and the main event on Wednesday night. What these three days reinforced is that hockey, more than any other professional North American team sport, is a players' sport. It is the players who control the ethos of the game—not the owners (quick, name one NHL owner), not the officials, not any hockey pop-culture icon, not the media (the ratings for the game ended up being dismal) and not the commissioner. Indeed, Commissioner Gary Bettman was booed upon being introduced in Dallas—a reception similar to the one given Texas Governor Rick Perry who, in a lame attempt to look hockey-like, dressed in a sleek, black, après-ski turtleneck (think "Banacek") as he dropped the all-star game puck. It was as incongruous as seeing Mitt Romney in a bolo tie and cowboy boots.

The game itself featured several innovations, the first being almost unthinkable in hockey circles: a fashion debut. Next year all NHL teams will be going to sleeker, more form-fitting and sweat-wicking jerseys, which were introduced to the public at the all-star game. This is seemingly a positive development for the players and perhaps for the sport as well until you visit the corn dog stand and picture the average hockey fan trying to squeeze into his new replica jersey. Perhaps the NHL's founders many decades ago were wise beyond their years when they chose "sweaters" as the players' attire.

This sartorial splendor was not matched by any corresponding tonsorial splendor. To the contrary, ever since helmets in NHL games became mandatory, grooming issues have proliferated. While the all-star game itself was a helmeted affair, the pregame festivities, the skills competition and practices were not, thus revealing that the "mullet" and the "Hanson brother" (*Slapshot*) are still acceptable 'do's in the NHL. Indeed, if Steve Nash had stuck to the national sport of his native Canada, he might be the George Clooney of the league.

·Mr. Hockey' – Gordie Howe

There was also a significant innovation in between-period entertainment. The NHL has always been challenged in this department because there are a limited number of things you can do on ice. Michael Jackson cannot pop up from beneath it. The diva du jour would have a difficult time walking across it in heels. And anything that is brought out between periods needs to be assembled, performed upon, and taken down in time to leave enough time for the Zamboni to resurface the ice. Thus, the American Airlines Center introduced (at least I hadn't seen it before) the "dropdown stage." Between periods, a stage descended from the rafters, a band performed, and then the stage was hoisted back up. Perhaps the most dramatic use of the stage was during the tribute to NHL legends on Monday night, when the stage was lowered displaying all sixteen trophies that are awarded annually by the NHL.

That sort of tradition was thick throughout the three days, and the NHL stars demonstrated a great respect for the game and acceptance of their role as ambassadors of the sport. Mr. Hockey himself, Gordie Howe, was conspicuous throughout the three days, both at the American Airlines Center and at the host hotel.

And when you think about the traditions of hockey, surely one of the names that pop into your mind first is . . . Cuba Gooding Jr.? It seemed like a strange choice of emcees for the "Salute to NHL Legends" event on Monday night, but he did a very creditable job and apparently is a huge hockey fan after rooming with a Canadian hockey player in college.

The selection of a Sunbelt city as the venue for the game provided several additional opportunities—one being the ability to have outdoor festivities surrounding the event (including bands and a reunion of the 1998–1999 Stanley Cup-winning Dallas Stars). It also provided a chance to highlight the growth of hockey as a result of the NHL's expansion. In 1993 when the Minnesota North Stars morphed into the Dallas Stars, there were no high school hockey teams in the Dallas area. Now there are 70, and the inclusion of youth and high school players in the events of the three days brought due attention to this fact. These themes will no doubt be repeated when the NHL All-Star Game moves to Atlanta next year.

All all-star games are more spectacle than sport, and this one was no exception, with the West winning 12–9. But the NHL would be well-served to harness and market around the respect the players have for the game and for each other, and their genuine willingness to be poster children for their sport.

# Being There Matters

Sidney Crosby, right, shakes Chris Osgood's hand

**October 2007** – You can just picture the scene of a couch potato somewhere in America groaning, "Nah, I'd rather just watch it from the comfort of my own living room," when asked if he would like to attend a major sporting event. But if you have this mind-set, you are missing a golden opportunity. You'll lose the chance to see the whole mosaic, rather than selected pieces. If you don't go, you are committed to a storyline being presented by the director of the broadcast, which is often from a preselected script, rather than watching the story unfold for yourself. It's the difference between viewing a documentary made by an art historian, as opposed to actually looking at a fine piece of art, directing more of your attention to the aspects of it that draw you in and interpreting it for yourself.

At an NBA game you can see for yourself the effort it takes to get open for a shot or to prevent your opponent from getting open—all work that takes place away from the ball and, therefore, away from the camera. When you're there, you can see the full scope of the minefield that Steve Nash navigates to create a play for one of his teammates, something that isn't captured on television, not even HDTV.

At an NFL game, you can marvel at a defensive lineman who gives 100 percent on every play rather than simply focusing on a lineman when he makes a big tackle. In tennis, you can see how tennis players conduct themselves between points and between games. You can see character revealed and tested. You can feel the spirit of the fans in the arena as well as the elevation of the human spirit when a competitor does something neither he, she nor we thought possible.

If there is one time when television coverage repeatedly lets me down, it's at the character-revealing moment of victory or defeat. In hockey, it's the Stanley Cup playoffs, when teams formally exchange handshakes at the end of the series. I watch this moment in person with intense interest. I watch to see how former teammates react to each other. I watch to see how formidable adversaries bury the hatchet. I watch to see the mutual respect of the people who play the same position, such as goalies. Television coverage often misses this golden opportunity to learn something about the competitors by instead showing random handshakes, or confetti raining down on the arena, or a player doing a unilateral exaltation, or the most superfluous camera shot of all: an outside aerial view of an indoor arena.

In tennis, the manner in which the victor and the vanquished approach the net and exchange greetings may tell me something about them. But if the camera cuts away to girlfriends, boyfriends, coaches or celebrities in the crowd, we miss pivotal parts of that moment that we wouldn't miss by being there. Is the body language frosty? Do the players make eye contact on their way to the net? The graciousness of Roger Federer comes out when you see him console early-round opponents, not just the better-known later-round ones.

In golf, what a moment it was in 1978 when Gary Player captured his final Masters, paired in the final round with a young Seve Ballesteros, who came running onto the green with a big beaming smile on his face to congratulate Player, a moment that the immediate television coverage at the time missed. But it said a lot about Ballesteros—and he would later say that one of the reasons he was so happy was that Player had just taught him how to win the Masters. Hey, there's no reason that magnanimity in defeat can't be coupled with just a little bit of self-interest.

I remember the tipping point in my sports-viewing career when I realized the frustrations of not being there. If I were Elvis, I might have been tempted to shoot out the television that night. It was October 17, 1994, and the Kansas City Chiefs were playing the Denver Broncos in a *Monday Night Football* game: an aging Joe Montana against John Elway. Montana was leading the Chiefs on a 75-yard drive at the end of the game that would culminate in a game-winning touchdown with eight seconds to play. It was one of his last showcase moments.

Had I been there, I would have been able to see the trademark Montana cool before, during and after each play and the response of his teammates. Instead, on TV after every single play, and I mean every single play, the camera cut to Jennifer Montana in the stands. I was watching this unfold at a sports bar with

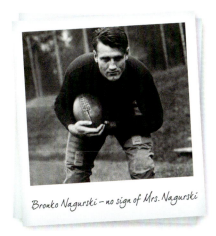

*Bronko Nagurski – no sign of Mrs. Nagurski*

a friend until I couldn't hold back. "Can you believe this?" I exclaimed. "Why do we have to constantly look at Jennifer Montana rather than what's happening on the field? I'll bet this didn't happen back in the day." I started to get a little carried away, veering far into the hypothetical. "I mean, can you imagine Bronko Nagurski running with the ball, and the camera constantly shifting to Mrs. Nagurski in the stands?" The retort of my buddy after hearing this diatribe? "Well, I'll bet Mrs. Nagurski didn't look like Mrs. Montana."

It was, no doubt, a valid point. But I don't care. Whether it is Mrs. Nagurski, Mrs. Montana or Gisele Bündchen and Bridget Moynahan sitting together at a Patriots game, I want to see what's on the field, and I want to direct my own coverage by attending the event in person. I have rarely regretted getting off the couch for it.

# CHAPTER 3
# TROUBLE AHEAD, TROUBLE BEHIND

# The Council of What?

*One third of the Council of Wisdom*

**August 2011** – Faced with multiple allegations of improprieties regarding soccer's international governing body, FIFA President Sepp Blatter did what many a sport or political leader before him has done: He formed a committee. But not just any committee. Blatter could have created something like cricket's "anti-corruption commission," a reassuring name that connotes something akin to Eliot Ness's "Untouchables." (As an aside, if your sport needs an ongoing "anti-corruption commission," the problem may be too endemic for a mere commission or committee to solve.) Instead, Blatter put a most curious and uniquely maladroit twist on the familiar "let's form a committee" concept.

The year 2011 has been particularly messy for Blatter, whose trail of problems stems back to his first election as FIFA President in 1998. His current travails include questions related to his 2011 re-election to a fourth term (a victory assured after his primary opponent removed himself from consideration after being accused of offering bribes), the suspension of four FIFA Executive Committee members, further allegations of bribery surrounding the selection of Qatar to host the 2022 World Cup, as well as controversy over the choice of Russia to host the 2018 World Cup. Amid calls to do something for soccer and FIFA's image, Blatter chose to form a "Council of Wisdom." And what sport luminaries would bring the "wisdom" to this council? None other than those noted soccer experts Placido Domingo and Henry Kissinger (along with former Dutch player Johan Cruyff). *Really?*

It would appear that Placido Domingo's primary involvement in soccer has been to sing at various soccer World Cups. But maybe Blatter is on to something. The traditional stewards of a number of sports seem to be having difficulties recently in dealing with various issues afflicting their competitions. So perhaps Blatter's theory that his sport's problems can be solved by a singer who has performed at one of sports' major events, teamed with a well-known international diplomat, should serve as a template for others.

*The Three Most Important People in the World*

For instance, Roger Goodell could have invoked Blatter's theory to solve the NFL labor problems by forming a commission composed of Christina Aguilera (whose performance at the most recent Super Bowl, although bungled, gives her the requisite experience) and former UN Secretary-General Kofi Annan. And what should the UCI do regarding Tyler Hamilton's very public allegations about doping in the Tour de France and other cycling events? A "Council of Substance" headed by Lady Gaga and former Secretary of State Madeleine Albright would be able to sort it all out.

What about problems with age verification in Little League baseball that surface every now and then? To minimize the risk of these occurrences, Little League would be well advised to form a "Council of Youth Wisdom" populated by Justin Bieber and child-star-turned-diplomat Shirley Temple Black—or even Rebecca Black, for that matter.

For competitions or leagues that are strictly domestic, we may not even need the international diplomat. As the NBA looks to address its own labor woes, a "Council of Greatness" headed by Spike Lee and Jack Nicholson (two of the most fervent celebrity observers of the game) would surely do the right thing—assuming the NBA could handle the truth. Perhaps they could even bring the "Octomom" into their council for her expertise on complicated labor issues.

But maybe I am selling Blatter short. Maybe his formation of a Council of Wisdom is moving us closer to the utopian future envisioned in the 1989 film *Bill and Ted's Excellent Adventure* in which society was ruled by a sort of Future Council made up of the Three Most Important People in the World. The chairman of that council was the late, great Clarence Clemons, who, of course would have been well qualified for any such position, having played a Super Bowl halftime show with the E Street Band. His two fellow council members were Fee Waybill, the lead singer of the Tubes, and Martha Davis, the lead singer of the Motels.

Whatever Blatter's intentions, his maneuver was as off pitch as the music of Wild Stallions—Bill and Ted's musical group that formed the basis for the civilization over which the Big Man, Waybill and Davis presided. Nevertheless, I do hope that the wisdom of Domingo, Kissinger and Cruyff can bring a better tone to international soccer governance.

# Tiger, Joe and Jack

Marilyn Monroe and Joe DiMaggio

**June 2010** – The return of the world's number one golfer and world's number one estranged husband (the latter title having more contenders than the former), freshly back to pro golf from sex rehab, certainly provided the leading story line to this year's Masters. I, like many, tuned in to see how Tiger 2.0 would differ from the original version. I certainly did not see any difference in temperament, as Tiger Woods struggled at times to find his rhythm (insert your own joke here).

It was hard to resist considering, once the tournament was over and Woods had finished fourth, whether his domestic relations affected his emotions on the course. I don't have the answer. Nor do I know what they teach in sex rehab. However, I do know this: As Tiger Woods tries to find his way forward, there are two available examples, one positive and one negative, he might consider to see how his life could end up.

The positive example is provided by the man Woods is chasing in Don Quixote–like fashion for the all-time record of major championships: Jack Nicklaus. Nicklaus has six green jackets to Woods's four, and 18 major championships to Woods's 14. Nicklaus also had and has one of the most extraordinary relationships and devotion to family of any professional athlete of his stature.

From all public accounts, Barbara Nicklaus was part of a true team with her husband during his pro career. Nicklaus would schedule golf tournaments around his family life, not the other way around. Was his success due in part to the fact that he married the girl from Clintonville, Ohio, he met during his first week at Ohio State University, and not the supermodel or starlet du jour? Hale Irwin certainly believed so when he said of Barbara Nicklaus, "Behind every good man is a better woman." That adage, however, is being tested in a time when sports, celebrity and entertainment get mixed together. The assumption is that once you reach a certain degree of prowess in professional sports, your spouse should be somebody who has achieved equal status in the acting, modeling, reality-show category. The new adage seems to be, "Behind every great athlete is a Kardashian sister."

Nicklaus himself may have realized how lucky he was, and where Woods might be heading, when he reportedly said after Woods's first Masters win: "The only thing that can stop him is a bad back or a bad marriage." Woods's template for fulfillment on the golf course and in family life need not be found in some unknown 12-step program, but rather in the example set by Nicklaus.

Now for the cautionary tale. Once upon a time there was another athlete—the marquee athlete of his generation—who married a glamorous blonde starlet and who, for all appearances, had everything going for him. In fact, Joe DiMaggio's 1954 marriage to Marilyn Monroe may have set the bar for modern-day athletes' personal aspirations. Even though the union lasted only nine months and was dissolved amid allegations of maltreatment by DiMaggio, it is still glamorized today.

The parallels between DiMaggio and Woods are striking. Consider this description of DiMaggio by Richard Ben Cramer in his definitive biography, *Joe DiMaggio: The Hero's Life*, published in 2000: "He was revered for his mystery. We cheered him for never giving himself entirely to us." Like the pre-November 2009 version of Woods, DiMaggio had a carefully cultivated public image during his playing career and spent his post-playing days as the keeper of his own legacy. As Cramer noted: "The coverage of DiMaggio over sixty-five years was mostly flat because Joe would show nothing but a shiny surface of his own devising" and would excommunicate anyone from his inner circle who would deign to reveal details of his life. Sound familiar?

To his dying day, DiMaggio was trying to find endorsement deals wherever he could—a path Tiger may be headed down if that creepy new Nike commercial is any indication. DiMaggio died a lonely death, with no supermodel, no starlet— aging or young—by his side, only a collection of carefully packaged memories.

Jack Nicklaus, by contrast, appears to be a fulfilled man. His extended family is close to him, and he and Barbara will celebrate their 50th anniversary this summer. There may be a lesson in that for Tiger Woods and for all professional athletes.

*Jack and Barbara Nicklaus*

After reading Cramer's book, I couldn't help but rethink one of Paul Simon's most inspired lyrics from the 1960s: "Where have you gone, Joe DiMaggio? A nation turns its lonely eyes to you." In the case of DiMaggio and Woods—unless he gets his act together soon—the nation could do better focusing on a role model more like Nicklaus.

# The Clear and the Cream

*A svelte Bonds in his Pirates years*

**June 2006** – As the 2006 baseball season gets under way, it's worth pausing for a moment to reflect upon how and why Barry Bonds has become the poster child of all that is wrong in sports. The label plastered on him most often is that of "cheat," but often lost in the debate are the specific grounds for such a characterization. Is it because he broke the rules of his sport? Is it because he broke the law? Is it because he tried to enhance his athletic performance in an artificial/chemical way? Any discussion of Bonds' legacy or his fitness for his sport's hall of fame, or any autopsy of his career, is complicated inordinately by the fact that until very recently, baseball had no anti-doping controls.

If an athlete uses substances that are (1) performance enhancing; (2) banned by the sport in which he competes; and (3) illegal, few would argue, absent extenuating circumstances, that the word "cheat" should not apply. However, when we start taking away elements of that trifecta, the issue becomes more cloudy.

What if an athlete is using substances that are illegal but are neither banned by a sport nor performance enhancing? The player whose home run record Bonds is about to surpass, Babe Ruth, hit many of his home runs during Prohibition. Yet his intake of alcohol was legendary. Certainly many an athlete has been associated with recreational illegal substances. Do such indiscretions automatically erase the athlete's career or any hope of getting into a hall of fame?

Bill Tilden is in the International Tennis Hall of Fame despite being convicted on morals charges. O.J. Simpson is in Canton despite being found responsible in civil court for two violent deaths. Bonds—unless his bulky frame suddenly expands in a crowded elevator and crushes the other occupants—has not quite reached that level of infamy.

An enlarged Bonds in his later Giants years

And what if an athlete uses substances that are performance enhancing but are not banned by his or her sport? In a recent commercial, Keith Jackson lauds the development of Gatorade at the University of Florida in the 1960s. Did the football players at the University of Florida who were drinking Gatorade have an advantage over their opponents who were drinking merely water on the other sideline? So says Keith Jackson.

One of the legendary moments in the Tour de France is the death of Tom Simpson on Mont Ventoux in 1967 with amphetamines in the pockets of his jersey. The Tour de France did not have any anti-doping controls at the time, so Simpson was not necessarily viewed as a "cheat." And Gatorade, far from being banned by sports, has been endorsed by athletes the world over. What is the difference between Gatorade and the "clear" and the "cream" that Bonds admits to taking? In the eyes of baseball at the time, the answer, unfortunately, is "nothing." The fact that the products with which Bonds is associated are performance enhancing may be insufficient in its own right to deny him his legacy.

What about the injection of substances that might be viewed as performance enhancing in one respect but are not taken for that purpose? I was recently called upon to draft a policy for allowing transgender athletes in competition, in the process encountering a word—"gonadectomy"—that I would have been happy to have gone the rest of my life without hearing.

In 2004, the International Olympic Committee paved the way for transgender athletes to compete in the Olympic games under a number of parameters, including the requirement that it be two years from an athlete's "gonadectomy." These transgender athletes may be taking substances that are banned by the sports in which they compete but are using them as part of the transgendering process rather than for performance enhancement (perhaps that's what Bonds was after when he dressed up as Paula Abdul for a "Giants Idol" gag during spring training).

In the context of sport, the primary reason for doping controls is not to enforce criminal statutes or morality or even to save athletes from the consequences of harmful substances. Rather, the rights holder's responsibility is to maintain a level playing field. When that doesn't happen, drawing a distinction between those who cheat and those who managed to find an "edge" is more difficult.

The National Baseball Hall of Fame itself is already populated with characters who skirted this line. Gaylord Perry is in the hall despite being strongly suspected on several occasions—and in fact being caught once—employing an illegal spitball.

But Perry's career began long after the spitball was outlawed, so perhaps a better analogy could be drawn between Bonds and those Hall of Famers who relied on the spitball before it was outlawed in 1920. Hall of Famer Burleigh Grimes, for example, whose career started before 1920 and who therefore was excepted from the "no spitball" policy, pitched for another 14 years, until 1934. Talk about an edge! Since Bonds's alleged use of performance-enhancing substances predates baseball's ban on them, the lens through which we should view his legacy is more creamy than clear.

# What's in a Name?

Chief Osceola and Renegade of Florida State University

**July 2006** – Throughout history, the mascot has been a symbol of the qualities that those who adopt it would like to possess, if only for the span of a sporting event. Lions and tigers and bears are a natural choice, and even less ferocious animals like horned frogs (TCU) and spiders (Richmond) have been claimed. For sheer terror in the hearts of opposing teams, surely nothing beats the name adopted by Hickman High in Columbia, Missouri—the Kewpies.

As long as animals or inanimate objects have been adopted as nicknames and mascots, they have served as a harmless way to identify a team. However, when Native American names are involved, controversy has followed. In August of last year, the NCAA approved a seemingly pragmatic process by which it would review the use of Native American mascots, nicknames and/or imagery at NCAA championships on a case-by-case basis. If a Native American mascot is deemed offensive, it is barred from display at any NCAA championship event and the school the mascot represents is barred from hosting any NCAA championship event.

In determining whether a mascot is offensive, the NCAA expressed its belief that the stereotyping of Native Americans is wrong, but recognized that Native American tribes are distinct political communities. If a particular tribe allows an institution to use its name and imagery, the NCAA will extend deference to the judgment of that tribe. Thus, schools that use a "namesake tribe" have a more identifiable route to acceptance than institutions that use a more generic nickname, such as Indians. Mississippi College was allowed to use its nickname,

Choctaws, because it received the approval of the Mississippi Band of Choctaw Indians. In perhaps the most publicized acceptance by the NCAA, Florida State received a blessing to retain the use of Chief Osceola as its mascot from Max Osceola, current chief and general council president of the Seminole Tribe of Florida.

The matter also gets a little tricky when a mascot may or may not be viewed as making reference to Native Americans. Such was the saga of the Fighting Illini of the University of Illinois. Does the mascot refer to a Native American tribe or to the State of Illinois? The NCAA went back and forth on the issue but concluded that it referred to a Native American tribe and was therefore subject to restriction, in the absence of any approval from the namesake tribe. Conversely, Merrimack College was allowed to retain its "Warrior" nickname because the image it used was that of a Spartan, as opposed to a Native American. There was no opposition from Sparta, nor is there likely to be, at least in the absence of a DNA experiment gone terribly wrong. Similarly, Bradley University was allowed to retain the nickname "Braves" on April 28 of this year, but only because it removed any Native American imagery associated with the name.

The NCAA's implementation of its policy on this potentially divisive issue has not been without its challenges. In the case of Florida State, the Seminole Tribe of Florida approved the use of "Seminoles," but the Seminole Nation of Oklahoma expressed its disapproval. The NCAA deferred to the Seminole Tribe of Florida. Since the NCAA's policy applies to national championships, the question can certainly be asked as to whether the NCAA should look to the "namesake tribe" solely within the home state of the institution that uses it.

In another confusing case, the NCAA received conflicting opinions regarding the University of North Dakota's use of the "Fighting Sioux" nickname from two different officials of the Standing Rock Sioux Tribe. Though some supported the use of the name, ultimately the view of those who opposed the use carried the day. Perhaps UND could have satisfied the wishes of all parties by changing its nickname to the "Fighting Sue," thereby risking rebuke only from the estate of Johnny Cash.

Without in any way diminishing the importance of the NCAA's efforts to address this very real issue, the academic question does arise as to whom deference might be shown for mascots not associated with Native American groups. What if there were conflicting viewpoints, for instance, on Rhode Island College's use of the nickname "Anchormen?" To whom would the NCAA turn? Katie Couric? For other mascots, there are obvious arbiters. In the case of the Furman University Purple Paladins the responsibility would surely fall to the most prominent member of purple nobility: the artist formerly and now again known as Prince. The Sweet Briar College Vixens? How about Ann Coulter? The Cal Poly and/or Hawaii Hilo Vulcans? Leonard Nimoy. The Whittier College Poets? Maya Angelou. And the Akron Zips (short for "zippers")? A certain former president comes to mind.

Nads T-shirt

Finally, no discussion of nicknames would be complete without mention of the Rhode Island School of Design hockey team, the "Nads." Ah, what better way to spend an afternoon than going to a hockey game and hearing supporters of the home team chanting "Go Nads!" Life would have been so much simpler if only we had stuck with lions and tigers and Kewpies.

# The Pursuit of Perfection

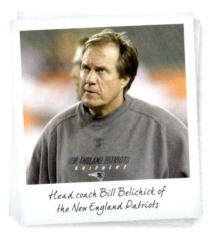
Head coach Bill Belichick of the New England Patriots

**February 2008** – As of press time, the New England Patriots have won more games—18—than any other NFL team in a single season. After completing an undefeated regular season, the Patriots are the odds-on favorite to win the Super Bowl and eclipse the 1972 Miami Dolphins' 17–0 perfect season with an even more impressive 19–0 run. But unlike those 1972 Dolphins—and the Green Bay Packers of the 1960s, the Boston Celtics of the 1950s and 1960s, the Chicago Bulls of the 1990s and most other American sports dynasties—the Patriots don't seem to have the overwhelming support of the sporting public as a result of this feat. I have been struggling to figure out why.

It certainly is not because Americans are anti-dynasty. Despite the "all men (and sports teams) are created equal" fervor that led to the founding of this country 232 years ago, we Americans still take a certain comfort in dynasties. In the political world, we elect presidents with the familiar last names of Adams, Roosevelt, Kennedy and Bush. In the sports world, we like to know who is truly at the top of the heap, and the masses turn out to see them.

But we also have a certain idea in our heads of what a dynasty should look like. And having seen football dynasties in the past, we even have a particular idea of what the leading figures in that dynasty should look like. When you are placing yourself among the greatest teams in the history of the sport, it's not enough to be just a "good quarterback" or a "good coach," as it would be if you were with simply a highly successful team. Rather, the bar gets raised to the level where the great historical figures in that sport have placed it. So, let's deconstruct the Patriots with that in mind.

Certainly, the league MVP, Tom Brady, is everything you would want in a football dynasty quarterback. He is Joe Montana and Joe Namath rolled into one person—the cool, calm, good-looking, workmanlike general on the field with a trail of supermodels off the field. Even if you aren't a Patriots fan, it is easy to root for Brady, a late bloomer who has blossomed into one of the greatest quarterbacks in the sport.

Similarly, the Patriots' defense is very much like the 1972 Dolphins' "no-name defense" (though the names of the "no-names" are now well-known). The Patriots' defense is greater than the sum of its parts but at the same time does bring well-deserved recognition to the talent of those parts. The fact that they place the team above individual accolades also makes them easy to root for. So there is no disconnect between the Patriots' defense and what we would perceive as a defense for the ages.

Not even Randy Moss—who this year broke Jerry Rice's record for touchdown receptions in a season, and whose background is spotted with controversies related to such things as illegal drugs, traffic incidents and violence allegations—is the focal point for those wanting to see a Patriots defeat. Every dynastic team needs a story of redemption. The fact that Moss now has some maturity to go along with his prodigious talent, coupled with America's infatuation with an outlaw-turned-icon story, makes him a net plus for Patriot fandom.

No, the character in the Patriots' drama that does not match the central casting version is the coach. Bill Belichick simply doesn't fit the mold of what we want in a football dynasty coach. Can you picture there someday being a "Bill Belichick Trophy" awarded to the AFC Conference champion or the Super Bowl champion similar to the Vince Lombardi and George Halas trophies? Lombardi, Halas, 1972 Dolphins coach Don Shula and San Francisco's Bill Walsh had character and countenances you could picture being chiseled onto Mount Rushmore. Belichick? Not so much. If Lombardi, Halas, Walsh, Shula and Belichick rushed the Delta House at Faber College, it would likely be Belichick who would be sent to the ancillary room with Mohammed, Jugdish, Sydney and Clayton—though he would no doubt find a way to spy on the real party through the walls.

Belichick as a coach suffers from what keeps many good players in any sport from being perceived as "great" players: He has no signature move, moment or innovation. His "moments" have often had tarnish associated with them— "Spygate," which cost his team their first round draft pick next year; his departure from the Jets to the Patriots, which was also punished by the NFL; and his undistinguished run as head coach of the Cleveland Browns. He hasn't brought about innovation like Walsh or Halas. Dressed in a hooded sweatshirt on game days, he hasn't cut the figure of Lombardi on the sidelines. The legendary voice of NFL Films, John Facenda, once said: "Lombardi. A certain magic still lingers in the very name. It speaks of duels in the snow and cold November mud."

*Vince Lombardi*

If the Patriots do win it all this year, it is still unlikely that any magic will linger in the name "Belichick" and he might be even better remembered by his nickname "Belicheat." How that affects the Patriots' legacy, only time will tell. But right now, it is most certainly the biggest reason for any lack of widespread public support for Patriot perfection.

# Heaven Can't Wait

Ted Williams's "temporary" resting place

**January 2007** – On a recent business trip to Scottsdale, Arizona, a colleague of mine and I finished our business early. Brainstorming ways to kill the time before our flight back to Dallas, inspiration hit us: "Aren't we close to that cryonics lab where Ted Williams is stored?" Indeed, a quick call confirmed that we were only half a mile away. Thus began a bizarre encounter with life or death—it is unclear which—in the twenty-first century.

Alcor Life Extension Foundation is housed in a nondescript office park. It was here that John Henry Williams and his sister Claudia chose to preserve the body and head, though reportedly not together, of their father, Ted Williams, after his death in 2002. The decision was made to the horror of Ted's daughter from a previous marriage, Bobby-Jo Williams Ferrell.

Ferrell wanted to cremate her father's body and sprinkle his ashes at sea as requested in Ted's 1997 will. But John Henry and Claudia cited a scrap of paper that had Ted Williams's signature on it, above which was written "JHW, Claudia and dad all agree to be put into biostasis after we die." The scrap of paper bears a date of November 2, 2000.

Whether this document should be given any legal effect, whether the writing above Ted Williams's signature was actually there when he signed the paper, and whether it truly reflected his intent, was the subject of a court battle that Ferrell was forced to abandon when it became too costly. Thus, the "Splendid Splinter" became the "Not-So-Splendidly Splintered"—a body and a head separately cryopreserved with liquid nitrogen in a giant cylinder. Bobby-Jo Ferrell alleged at the time of Ted Williams's death that it was John Henry's intention to cryopreserve their father's body in order to sell his DNA. As Barbaro will hopefully come to realize, there are much better ways of being put out to stud.

That the great Ted Williams should end up like this—a punch line to modern cultural times—is tragic. Mark Twain once said "I am not *an* American; I am *the* American." Twain was actually referring to what Frank Fuller, the governor of Utah, had said, but because it fit Twain so perfectly he has been regarded as "the" American of the nineteenth century. If I had to choose "the" American of the twentieth century, it would be Ted Williams. Twain wrote the great American novel. Williams lived the great American novel—he was the greatest hitter in the great American sport.

Like Twain—a novelist, raconteur, newspaperman, steamboat captain and miner—Williams excelled in more than one field. Williams possessed world-class skills in three disciplines: baseball, fishing and aviation. He was a decorated fighter pilot in both World War II (after hitting .406 in 1941) and the Korean War. He lost five years of baseball to service for his country, yet still ended his career third on the all-time home run list.

A more dignified display
of Ted Williams's head

Also like Twain—whose writings reflect his life spent in Missouri, California, Connecticut and other places—Williams can't be associated with just one American location. He was raised in San Diego, played baseball in Boston and spent his later years in Florida, where, if his will had been given effect, his ashes would have been scattered off the coast.

If Williams was indeed "the" American of the twentieth century, perhaps his greatest mistake was living into the twenty-first century, where family feuds, legal disputes, dubious notes on scratch paper, thoughts of selling DNA, and suspension of bodies and heads in shared cylinders in office parks have become the order of the day. Twain once quipped, while living in London: "Reports of my death are greatly exaggerated." John Henry and Claudia Williams were apparently hoping this could be their father's epitaph on his tank in Scottsdale.

We had no plans as to what to do upon arrival at Alcor. The door was closed. We rang the bell and a woman opened the door. I began to diplomatically explain that we were interested in the operation of their facility. My colleague had a slightly different and less subtle approach: "We're here to see Ted's head," he said. To my everlasting surprise, the woman let us in. As you enter the facility, the pictures of Alcor's 73 cryopreserved "patients" are on the wall with plaques underneath them. Thus, for example, you would see, "John Doe—First Lifecycle 1958–2001." I began to feel like a load of laundry, more than halfway through my own first "cycle."

A few steps into the facility is a mock-up of how a "patient" is cryopreserved. We were then greeted by a man who, if he wasn't the crypt keeper, certainly could have been a stand-in. We asked a few questions. No, we can't see the patients. But yes, we are ideal patients ourselves, with enough tread on our tires in our first "life cycle" to be able to enjoy the fruits of life in the twenty-fourth century or whenever we would be reanimated. If we wanted our whole bodies cryopreserved, it would cost a clean $150,000. Just our brains would be a mere $80,000.

After learning all we need to know about the cryo game (my apologies to Boy George) we'd had enough. Yes, we shared a few chuckles on the way out, hopefully at the surreality of the situation and not at the expense of the memory of Ted Williams. It would have been much more befitting if I'd thought of him as I looked out over the Florida Keys rather than a nondescript office park in Scottsdale.

# Don't Forget the Game

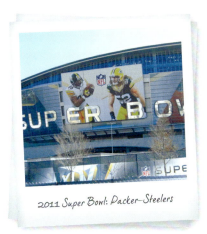

2011 Super Bowl: Packer–Steelers

**March 2011** – For the second straight February, Jerry Jones tried to set an attendance record at an American professional sporting event: the NBA All Star Game last year at Cowboys Stadium and the Super Bowl this year. For the second straight February, Diddy decided to grace Dallas with his presence and host a celebrity-filled bash in the days before the game. And for the second straight February, uncharacteristic, crippling winter weather descended upon Dallas. God does not like Jerry Jones or Diddy, or both. Jones also had to pay another penance: He had to live for a week with the logos of the dreaded Steelers and Packers on his cathedral.

The gaffes associated with this year's Super Bowl have been well documented. In addition to the monumental ones, such as some ticket holders being turned away, there were silly little annoyances as well. For instance, the only exit from the main souvenir shop required an exit and re-entry to the stadium. Equally as puzzling was a "martini bar" inside the stadium that was supplied only with vodka, no vermouth. "How does this martini bar differ from a shot bar?" I asked. "I guess it doesn't," confessed its proprietor. Perhaps it took its inspiration from Diddy's Super Bowl party where the only nutrition was Ciroc-vodka-infused lemon cupcakes, as an homage to Diddy's favorite drink (or so I was told): vodka and lemonade. Who knew?

These issues disguise the more fundamental problem of what the Super Bowl has become. Of the four leading American team sports, football is the only one for

*Diddy at his Super Bowl party*

which we know exactly where and when the champion will be crowned. This leads all those who crave an enhanced cultural profile to flock to that place and create an orgy of celebrity that dwarfs the actual game.

The other problem is that the Super Bowl exists for the 111 million television viewers rather than the 100,000 fans who actually attend the game. If you don't believe that, do you think the military flyover above a domed stadium was for the 100,000 fans in attendance? I can assure you that we were unmoved by it, since we didn't see it.

This is not a new phenomenon. It has been this way since the first Super Bowl when the Green Bay Packers were forced to kick off a second time to start the second half because the TV production had not returned from a commercial in time. (If you wonder why Vince Lombardi agreed to such an intrusion by television into the actual football competition, the Kansas City Chiefs had secured fairly good field position on the initial kickoff.)

I hate to single out any one Super Bowl ritual for absurdity, but Media Day at the Super Bowl has to be one of the most inane creations of our time. Joe Namath makes a bold statement 42 years ago, lightning is captured in a bottle, and now we devote an entire day trying to make the same thing happen again. I've had more enlightenment watching *Jersey Shore* than I have had from Media Day at the Super Bowl—or so I thought until I encountered a well-fueled Mike "The Situation" Sorrentino at the *Sports Illustrated*/Black Eyed Peas' party the Friday before the Super Bowl.

It's impossible during Super Bowl week not to encounter NFL players past and present at every turn. There was Jim McMahon hosting a party, billing himself as "two-time Super Bowl champion." Really? Being on the sideline for the Green Bay Packers in 1997 is on par with leading the Bears to victory in 1986? There was Jets quarterback Mark Sanchez, five points away from playing in the Super Bowl himself, at the Diddy party, though the paparazzi showed more photographic interest in the Avion Tequila girls than Sanchez. What a difference five points can make. And there was Earl Campbell at the Media Party, plopped down on a couch, looking like Buddha, as various admirers took their turns posing for pictures next to him while he mumbled niceties into their ear.

Amidst all this, there were many pleasant surprises and rewarding moments, but all of them were football related. I may have been one of the few out of 103,000 who actually had a good time at the game. The Packers against the Steelers proved to be a great match-up, and it was inspiring watching Aaron Rodgers establish himself as the real A-Rod, not the guy who was up in a box having popcorn placed into his mouth by Cameron Diaz.

Once the game started, Cowboys Stadium was a dramatic place to watch the action, made so by the number of ardent Steelers and Packers fans who made the trek to Texas. I had always thought that the Hollywood glitterati and corporate guests who attended Super Bowls would sit on their hands, ruining any ambiance of the game. For this one at least, I was wrong. Regardless of which team had the ball there were tens of thousands of their real supporters in the stands, including Carol, the Packers' season ticket-holding grandmother in my section who warned me before the opening kickoff that she would be screaming her head off throughout the game. She did. She also confided that she had been on five "Packer cruises" to the Caribbean and confessed, "I've played bingo with Aaron Rodgers." If she knew her bingo as well as her football, Aaron was in trouble. Carol paid her way to the Super Bowl by winning her fantasy football league.

These are the fans who make a Super Bowl. And these are the fans who seem to have gotten lost in the NFL's Super Bowl planning. Perhaps the substantial screw-ups and the disenfranchised ticket holders at this year's game will refocus the NFL on the real fans out there who want the Super Bowl to be about football, not pop culture. When our tendencies arise to blow the game out of proportion, the words of Cowboys running back Duane Thomas before the 1972 Super Bowl in response to a question about whether this was the "ultimate game" come to mind: "If it's the ultimate game, how come they're playing it again next year?"

# Just Don't Bring Your Guitar

McEnroe on guitar

**February 2011** – Ah, my sister. You gotta love her. Knowing my twin loves of sports and music, she combined them in a Christmas gag gift: the 2005 CD *Oh Say Can You Sing?*, which features songs performed by Major League Baseball players. As recording artists, these guys are very good baseball players—though Ozzie Smith's rendition of Sam Cooke's "Cupid" is oddly compelling. I will, however, give them all a pass since they were doing it for fun and charity. While the performances are, for the most part, not terrible, none of the players would advance far on *American Idol*. By the same token, don't expect to see Susan Boyle playing outfield for the New York Yankees anytime soon.

And there is a reason for that. It is best explained in John McEnroe's autobiography, *You Cannot Be Serious*. As his tennis career was winding down, McEnroe toyed with the idea of becoming a rock musician, as did other of his tennis-playing contemporaries such as Mats Wilander, Pat Cash and Yannick Noah—with Noah actually becoming a very popular act in France before he became even more famous in America for fathering the center of the Chicago Bulls. McEnroe, however, had the good fortune to marry a rock star, Patty Smyth, who one day sat him down and gave him a reality check on his talent: "The Lord doesn't let you be one of the greatest tennis players that ever lived and then be Keith Richards. It just doesn't work that way." Similarly, the thought of Keith Richards playing Wimbledon doesn't work either.

The MLB album reminded me of the legions of athletes who attempt, seriously, to embark on second careers as musicians, expecting to get the same adoration they had as athletes. Perhaps they are driven by the thought: "Hey, I put a lot of dedication and hard work into becoming a pro athlete, so if I do the same thing in another field I will get the same results." Some may see it as a way of enhancing or maintaining their celebrity; some might be trying to summon up the adrenaline rush they had as athletes; and some simply may be padding an outsized ego. Whatever the motivation, the Smyth Doctrine is largely intact.

Certainly the nadir of the athlete-turned-singer was Carl Lewis's massacre of the national anthem in 1993. Also in the National Anthem category, I recently saw gymnast Carly Patterson, whose 2009 debut album *Back to the Beginning* was undistinguished, do disservice to the tune.

Shaquille O'Neal was on the forefront of a wave of NBA stars who tried to reinvent themselves as rappers with *Shaq Diesel* and *Shaq Fu—Da Return*, which the usually reliable website allmusic.com charitably describes as showcasing Shaq's "moderate rapping talents." Of course, with the rivalry between Shaq and Kobe Bryant, Kobe could not resist the temptation to put out his own rap album, *K.O.B.E.*, which still awaits the acclaim of a grateful nation, as do Ron Artest's *My World* and a host of others.

Oscar de la Hoya: a long-lost Bee Gee?

Then, of course, there is the inexplicable. What, for instance, prompted Oscar de la Hoya to do a cover version of the Bee Gees' "Run To Me" complete with an amazingly cheesy musical video that is available on YouTube?

There are some limited exceptions to the Patty Smyth theory. Jack McDowell of the Chicago White Sox and his band V.I.E.W., which was the opening act for a Smithereens tour in the '90s, might fall into this category. Allmusic.com describes V.I.E.W., which later morphed into Stickfigure, as "generally decent"—not particularly high praise, but certainly moving from mere musical proficiency to professionalism, a distinction far too many athletes ignore.

The greatest historical athlete-entrant into musical professionalism might be Paul Robeson, who is in the College Football Hall of Fame and whose performance of "Ol' Man River" in 1936 remains the definitive version of the song.

If there is one genre of music where athlete-musicians have been more viable, it would be in smooth jazz. Former New York Yankees center fielder Bernie Williams was nominated for a Latin Grammy for his 2009 album *Moving Forward* and the late, great basketball player Wayman Tisdale hit No. 1 on the contemporary jazz chart in 2001 with "Face to Face."

Most athletes considering a foray into a musical career, however, might be wise first to consult another vignette from McEnroe's book, which is refreshingly self-effacing—and in line with the advice Smyth would eventually give him. McEnroe tells a story that took place at Wimbledon in 1982. In his early days of learning the guitar, he would use downtime between rounds of a tournament to tinker with the instrument. On this occasion, he was in his hotel suite working on David Bowie's "Suffragette City" and "Rebel Rebel" when someone knocked on his door. It was none other than Bowie himself. "Come up and have a drink," Bowie said. "Just don't bring your guitar."

# A Matter of Antitrust

**July 2011** – It is hard to be a fan of American football these days without hearing the word "antitrust." In college football, as of this writing, Utah Attorney General Mark Shurtleff is threatening an antitrust suit against the Bowl Championship Series, contending that the BCS system is an illegal monopoly by the major conferences that restricts the ability of teams like the University of Utah and Boise State to reach the BCS title game and share in the riches that such a game brings (never mind that Utah is moving to the Pac-12 this fall).

Meanwhile, in professional football, on March 11, 2001, the day the collective bargaining agreement between the NFL and the players union expired and the players were "locked out" by the owners, Tom Brady and ten other players sued the NFL, alleging antitrust violations. Thus, to help football fans who did not take antitrust law in law school (who, I assume, make up approximately 99.999 percent of the NFL's fan base), I will take a stab at trying to explain this new landscape.

**So what is antitrust law anyway?** Antitrust law came into being around the turn of the last century to try to prevent monopoly power and ensure competition in the marketplace. Some of the words in the Brady lawsuit are words that are commonly used when someone is alleging violation of the antitrust laws: "Unlawful group boycott," "price fixing arrangement," "anti-competitive restrictions."

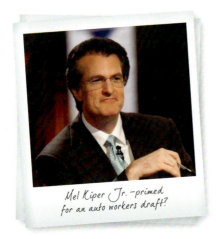
Mel Kiper Jr. –primed
for an auto workers draft?

**How can anyone claim that the NFL is anti-competitive when it has 32 teams trying to beat each other's brains out every fall weekend?** Sports leagues are an interesting beast when it comes to antitrust law. Is the NFL, for instance, a single entity that competes against other sports—MLB, NBA, NHL, NASCAR—or is it 32 entities that compete against each other, or is it both? After all, if it is a single entity, it would be hard to stage a "group" boycott with itself. Also, activity that might seem anti-competitive in the business arena actually may be viewed as enhancing competition in the sports arena. For instance, could you imagine General Motors and Ford agreeing to do a draft of entry-level workers each year in which the chosen worker does not decide where to go? (The thought of Mel Kiper Jr. offering his punditry on auto workers is chilling.) In sports, however, entry-level drafts and free agent movement are viewed as necessary for competitive balance.

**Well then, shouldn't antitrust laws really just apply to businesses and not to sports?** Ah, but where does sport end and business start? This brings us to one of the great anomalies in American law. In 1922, the United States Supreme Court held in the case of *Federal Baseball Club of Baltimore v. National League* that Major League Baseball was exempt from antitrust law because baseball was a game, not a business. Perhaps you can use that argument to bargain with your local team next time you get your bill for your season tickets. However, the Supreme Court chooses the cases it takes, and for the last 89 years no one has wanted to be the Supreme Grinch who killed baseball's antitrust exemption, even as the business of baseball and other sports has grown exponentially. Congress has always had the power to do something about baseball's antitrust exemption by drafting legislation that would specifically state that antitrust laws apply to baseball. In fact, it is the threat of Congress creating such a law that led MLB to cooperate in matters like the infamous steroid hearings before Congress.

**So wouldn't the Supreme Court have to decide a case involving the NFL or the BCS the same way?** Maybe not. Supreme Court decisions are "forever" in the same sense that when Elizabeth Taylor married it was forever. The Latin phrase is *stare decisis* which, loosely translated, means that the Supreme Court is not supposed to flip-flop. In reality, the Court has made some historic flip-flops such as deciding in 1896 that there was nothing unlawful about racially segregated schools and then 58 years later in *Brown v. Board of Education* deciding that it was wrong. So no, the Supreme Court could decide the football cases differently, though it is questionable whether antitrust law as applied to sports is worth reconsidering the way school desegregation was.

**So what's going to happen with the NFL and the BCS?** While there may be some scrimmages in the lower courts, it is unlikely that the Supreme Court will jump into this dispute. For one thing, Supreme Court justices are humans too and most are football fans (in Supreme Court lore, Washington Redskins tickets are a valuable commodity). No one is eager for a major legal decision that decides once and for all the antitrust parameters for professional sports leagues. Look for a negotiated solution to both the NFL and BCS issues.

Class over. Enjoy the rest of your summer vacation.

# Presentation Breakdown

Nadal and Djokovic enduring the awards presentation

**March 2012** – Award ceremonies following a sports championship can make for awkward moments. The phone call from the President of the United States to the manager of the winning World Series team after the deciding game generally displays as much camaraderie and genuineness as a phone call from a telemarketer. Then there is the executive of a sponsor or organization who takes the opportunity to give ill-conceived analysis of what just took place on the playing field. And there is always the general feeling that we are watching an imposition on the contestants' time, with the winners wanting to celebrate and the losers wanting to commiserate with the people closest to them.

But the awards presentation at this year's Australian Open may have been the most uncomfortable I have ever seen. Novak Djokovic and Rafael Nadal had played five of the most physical sets of tennis imaginable, with Djokovic needing almost six hours to capture the title—a record playing time for a Grand Slam final. These are two of the fittest athletes on the planet, but they could barely stand up by the end of the match—a fact that was obvious to all in attendance, with the apparent and unfortunate exception of people given a microphone for the awards presentation. A representative from Kia and the president of Tennis Australia each droned on for what seemed like hours while Djokovic and Nadal alternated between wobbling from side to side, squatting, bending over and grabbing their ankles to keep from cramping, and ultimately leaning back against the net for support. The two speakers meanwhile spoke in halting sentences, with those annoying pauses to invite applause that is given only because it would be impolite to do otherwise.

ESPN's Chris Fowler spoke for all of us watching on television, when he noted that Djokovic and Nadal would each be willing to forfeit some of their prize money if the speeches could be shortened. Finally, when the speakers were close to finishing anyway, some alert official came out with chairs for Djokovic and Nadal, to massive applause from the crowd—every single member of which noticed the situation, while the presenters remained oblivious.

As I was watching this scene unfold, the frustration in me caused me to imagine what might have happened if the two contestants suffering through this were not two of the most gracious athletes in the game but rather, say, John McEnroe and Jimmy Connors. McEnroe at best would have walked off the court. Connors would have been more likely to grab the microphone and say: "Excuse me, but I have to get to the locker room, thank you very much for coming."

1983 World Series MVP Rick Dempsey telling President Reagan: "You can tell the Russians that we're having an awfully good time over here playing baseball."

The Australian Open presenters violated realization No. 1 for awards presenters at a sports championship: No one came to watch you present. It is not your moment, it is the athlete's moment. Enhance it; don't detract from it. And there has never been a presentation where brevity was not appreciated.

Each of these presenters, by staying with their prepared, bland, and deliberately delivered remarks, missed a golden opportunity to enhance their brands. Imagine if the Kia guy had come out and said: "We at Kia try to be responsive to our customers' needs, and right now I want to be responsive to the needs of these two great players, that being to get into the locker room. So may I just say congratulations to each of them for a great tournament." And how would attendees and viewers feel about Tennis Australia if its president had then said: "Well, I want to follow suit. At Tennis Australia we are all about the players and right now it should be all about these two players, who gave a performance for the ages. So I will simply say thank you to everyone involved in the tournament and thank you to our champion and runner-up." That would have taken about forty seconds between them.

One of my favorite demonstrations of a presenter or speaker knowing his place occurred when a friend of mine was called upon to introduce the keynote speaker at a gathering of an organization to which we both belonged. The president of the organization was to introduce my friend who was then to introduce the speaker; thus there, potentially, would be two speeches before the audience heard the speech they came to hear. The president introduced my friend with the usual, monotonous recitation of his accomplishments. My friend then took the podium and said simply: "Ladies and gentlemen, Rod Jones." Rod Jones (not his real name, lest other presenters in the future do the same thing to him!) began his presentation with a big smile on his face and said: "That's the best introduction I've ever had." And he meant it. The audience felt the same way.

# CHAPTER 4

# LEARNING FROM THE GAME

# Sports Science

*San francisco Giants win 2010 World Series*

**December 2010** – The San Francisco Giants' World Series victory has reinforced that a particular discipline of science has progressively crept into the sports consciousness. The Giants did not have an everyday position player who was an acknowledged superstar. That's sometimes the way it goes in American sports. Either a team rides the back of a superstar to a championship or comes together as a team of equals, misfits (the Giants) or "idiots" (Johnny Damon's description of his 2004 Boston Red Sox). When a team takes this latter route to a championship, it is inevitable that every description of that team lauds its "chemistry."

But how did chemistry hijack the sports page from other academic departments, including other science departments? After all, what happens when a bat hits a ball is much more a product of physics than chemistry. And elements such as a player's size and speed, not to mention the much-coveted ability to pitch left-handed, are matters of biology, not chemistry. It amazes me that, in the competitive world of academia, the physics and biology departments have ceded this sports ground to the chemistry department.

When we speak of team chemistry, of course, what we really are making reference to are intangibles like team members being inspired to play for each other, to bring out the best in each other, and to create a situation where the whole is greater than the sum of the parts (a proposition with which the math department may take issue). But when we analyze the way players interact with each other, aren't we talking more about sociology than chemistry? Staying in the social science field for a moment, many teams employ sports psychologists. If chemistry is more critical to on-field performance, why don't sports teams employ team chemists?

There is, of course, the irony of citing the triumphs of chemistry in sports, particularly in the sport of baseball, at a time when concerns about performance-enhancing substances are so pervasive. Perhaps this is one reason you do not often hear of a cycling team in the Tour de France having good team "chemistry." Such a quote from a team member in a French newspaper is likely to be misinterpreted and result in an immediate raid of the team's hotel rooms by French authorities.

I also am surprised that theology departments do not step in and take some degree of credit. With the number of players who, in postgame interviews, attribute their performance to God, Jesus or both, it is somewhat incongruous that we do not hear about good "team theology." Perhaps theology professors have heeded the words of Yogi Berra, who reportedly said, after Minnie Minoso stepped into the batter's box and made the sign of the cross, "Minnie, don't you think God should be allowed to just watch the game?" Come to think of it, shouldn't the philosophy department stand up for itself? Given the phenomenal postseason success of the philosopher Berra, it would seem that philosophy would deserve some credit. Plus, as the eloquent Mr. Berra once observed of baseball, "90 percent of this game is half mental."

With all the statistical analysis and metrics in baseball, such as a player's batting average against right-handed pitchers in night games when the temperature is below 55 degrees, mathematicians should be particularly incensed about the credit given to chemistry. Math was even at the forefront of one of sports' great controversies when Colorado beat Missouri en route to the National Championship of college football in 1990 by scoring on fifth down when the referees lost track of downs. And let's not forget the literature department in this analysis either. The success of Giants pitcher Tim Lincecum may be attributed to his adoption of the pitching delivery of the fictitious Sidd Finch.

Perhaps it is not the examples of positive team chemistry but rather the negative examples of a radioactive mix of players, or the bringing in of an unstable element, that brings the focus to chemistry. The toxic Randy Moss, now with his third team in just half a football season, is a prime example. The Minnesota Vikings put him on waivers and only one team in the league, the Tennessee Titans, picked him up. Thus, it is perhaps the detonator—not the catalyst—that is responsible for the toehold chemistry has had in the sports lexicon for so many years.

A unique chemistry experiment may be taking place this basketball season as we all watch the beaker of LeBron James, Dwayne Wade and Chris Bosh interact with the Miami Heat. If the amalgamation of three superstars with only one basketball between them works, will it be a tribute to chemistry or alchemy?

Chris Bosh, Dwayne Wade and LeBron James. Chemically bonded or strange brew?

I, for one, would like to see more parity in the credit allocated to various academic disciplines for the performance of a sports team. It is high time to convene the academic roundtable and figure out the appropriate curricular mix for maximum team performance.

# When Youth Sports Go Pro

The DiMaggio doctrine is being challenged

**November 2006** – Joe DiMaggio once said, "A ball player has to be kept hungry to become a big leaguer. That's why no boy from a rich family has ever made the big leagues." Mr. DiMaggio, meet Kenny Troutt. Troutt, founder of Excel Communications, has one son in third grade and one son in fifth grade, and the Dallas billionaire funds traveling basketball teams for both of them, complete with private jets, full-time coaches, nutritionists and numerous other support staff. But to what end? To try to prove Joltin' Joe wrong? To try to live a parent's fantasy through children? To provide opportunities that would not otherwise exist?

Indeed, his two teams do include kids from disadvantaged backgrounds, leading some to laud Troutt's efforts. But in such an environment, do kids have a chance to be kids and to learn the lessons they need to learn in childhood?

The professionalization of children's sports is becoming rampant. The "2005 Youth Sports National Report Card" from the Citizenship Through Sports Alliance gave a telling evaluation of youth sports in the United States. The CTSA, which is committed to promoting positive behavior in youth sports, evaluated youth sports programs serving children age 6–14 in five areas, with the following grades being given to each: Child centered philosophy, D; Coaching, C-; Health & Safety, C+; Officiating, B; Parental Behavior/Involvement, D.

That's right: the officials, while enduring chants of "kill the ump," scored the highest of anyone involved in youth sports, with a B. At the bottom of the food chain are parents, who are responsible for propagating a parent-centered approach to youth sports rather than a child-centered one.

I doubt Joe DiMaggio would have extrapolated his 1930s economic analysis to the psychoanalysis of the early 2000s, but I will. It may no longer be necessary for a kid to go hungry in order to have the drive to become a pro athlete, but I'm not sure the DiMaggio doctrine is dead. The growing number of foreign-born Major League Baseball players, especially from Latin America, might indicate that it is still viable.

What any child needs to succeed in sports is to have a sense of owning the moment. Perhaps what DiMaggio meant is that kids from poor families learn to develop a sense of striving for themselves and thereby owning their own moments. Every great athlete and, in fact, every successful person in any field, develops a sense of owning the moment. However, in a youth sports culture where parental and benefactor involvement is dominant, do kids develop that sense?

Brooks Johnson, the great track coach, once said, "If you want to see a runner with great technique, watch a kid," before all the handlers get to him. A third grader with an entourage may not only be compromising his psychological development—learning to own the moment—but he also may not be developing his physical skills in a natural way.

One of my first vivid youth sports memories happened when I was 10 years old and playing Little League baseball. The dominant pitcher in the league was a 12-year-old, Dominic Tedesco, who would later play defensive end at Michigan. He was 12 and prematurely studly. I was 10 and prematurely undersized.

Without adult intervention, I figured out for myself that the only way I could have a chance against him was to use an even lighter bat than usual. Naturally the defense was playing every batter who faced him to swing late, shifting heavily to right field. So I also opened my stance—again, without any coach or parent telling me to do so. Tedesco did exactly what he should have done with a puny 10-year-old, which was to throw a high inside fastball. With my lighter bat, I managed to get around on it and pull it down the third base line. By the time the shifted defense got to the ball, I was standing on third with a triple.

After the game, I hopped on my bike and went to Baskin-Robbins, where I had a double mint chocolate chip in a sugar cone with my teammates. I can still, decades later, remember the taste of that cone. Then I got on my bike and rode home. No plane, no adults, no swing coaches, and certainly no nutritionist telling me to lay off the mint chocolate chip. It was my moment—thinking, acting and reacting on my own. I later would move from baseball to other sports, but that experience and that feeling of being in the moment stayed with me.

Do the kids on Kenny Troutt's teams have moments like that? I hope so. But when the parents and professional coaches and trainers and nutritionists and traveling secretaries and skills instructors are involved, I'm not sure how it is possible for a kid to learn how to own a moment. When parents and handlers cover all the bases for their young athletes, places and situations may all seem the same to the young mind, and the magic of the moment is lost on them. I picture the third grader on Troutt's team kind of like the rock star in the Southwest Airlines commercial who says "Hello Cleveland!" only to be met by silence, which is broken by one of his bandmates whispering, "Cleveland was last night."

```
Dear Bob,

Yesterday I came across your article "When Youth Sports Go Pro". I
enjoyed reading your perspective and am delighted to know  I am part
of your "most vivid youth sports memories", and that I helped you
"own the moment".

Personally, I would have left Indian Gardens and gone to 31 Flavors
for a double dip of Oregon Blackberry and Lemon Custard, but it
wasn't my moment. Hope all is well with you.

Best wishes and warmest regards,

Dominic Tedesco
```

*After this piece appeared, I received this gracious communiqué from Dominic Tedesco, who I had not heard of or from in decades – an incidental benefit of writing a monthly column.*

# Putting in a Good Word

*Josh Hamilton*

**August 2008** – I was reading Albert Chen's cover story in *Sports Illustrated* on the remarkable comeback of baseball player Josh Hamilton, and I was struck by two vignettes in the story. Hamilton was the first pick in the 1999 baseball draft, but he subsequently battled drug addiction, was out of baseball completely for three years, and didn't make it to the major leagues until last year. In a remarkable tale of prodigious talent wasted followed by redemption and resurrection, what stood out to me were the comments of support that Hamilton received when he finally made it to the major leagues.

Chen cites two such examples. The first was Hamilton's first major league at-bat at home in Cincinnati when opposing catcher Michael Barrett of the Chicago Cubs said to Hamilton during the ovation he was receiving: "Congratulations, Josh. You deserve it. Take it all in." Later in the season, after Hamilton had reached second base during a game against the Houston Astros, Craig Biggio made reference to a former teammate who had battled substance abuse. "I knew Ken Caminiti. I know how hard it is, but you're headed in the right direction. Good going."

Hamilton has been one of the season's biggest comeback stories. In addition to being a contender for the Triple Crown, he hit a record 28 home runs in the opening round of the All-Star Game's Home Run Derby, winning over the Yankee Stadium crowd.

In an era of public braggadocio and private trash talking, it sometimes can be lost how encouraging words from a teammate or, even more powerfully, from an opponent can mean a great deal to an athlete. Obviously the two comments above had a profound effect on Hamilton for him to have shared them with the writer.

Luz Long and Jesse Owens during the 1936 Olympics

Perhaps the most famous example of words of support offered by a competitor took place during the 1936 Olympics in Berlin when German long jumper Luz Long offered advice to Jesse Owens after Owens had fouled on his first two attempts in the long jump. The suggestion by Long helped Owens qualify for the long jump finals, and he would go on to win the gold medal, with Long winning the silver. Not only had Long helped a competitor but he had done so as a German, in full view of Adolf Hitler, to an African American.

Josh Hamilton is only 27, but the comments he received from Barrett and Biggio (and others that he might receive from opposing players) will increase in importance over time. The scores of games, the standings, the statistics all fade in memory. At the end of the day what remains are the friendships, relationships and human moments an athlete experiences as a result of his involvement in sports.

As Jesse Owens himself wrote of his experience with Luz Long, "You could melt down all the medals and cups I have and they wouldn't be a plating on the 24-karat friendship that I felt for Luz Long." Long died in World War II, but Owens continued to stay in touch with his family for the rest of his own life.

In late 1992, the season before he retired from baseball, Nolan Ryan had an encounter with Randy Johnson in which he suggested that Johnson make a slight change in his pitching delivery. The next year, 1993, Johnson struck out 300 batters for the first time and finally began to make the most of his talent. Johnson to this day gives Ryan credit for elevating his game.

Ryan has been retired from baseball for 15 years, and Randy Johnson will reach retirement soon. They might have been sitting on each other's porch swings in the future, comparing strikeout-to-walk ratios had not Ryan sought out Johnson and offered his positive influence. Instead, those porch-swing conversations over the next 30 years will be much more meaningful.

Such words of encouragement need not be limited to major league ballparks and Olympic stadiums, or even to adults or professionals. I have a very distinct memory of a time when I was 11 years old, playing my first nationally ranked tennis opponent. I held my own, but my inexperience was my undoing. My opponent, who was one year my senior, took several minutes after the match to make a couple of helpful suggestions that his coach had made to him and he thought might help me out in the future. I don't remember the score of the match or the playing conditions, but to this day I do remember those helpful suggestions word for word.

I am in no way suggesting that we be cheerleaders for our opponents. Nor am I against the well-phrased or well-delivered provocative comment to an opponent. (And indeed, I reserve the right in a future column to reveal some of my all-time favorites in this category!) But when you have a chance to express a heartfelt thought or friendly support to an opponent, don't necessarily be deterred because he or she is wearing a different uniform. The uniforms will shrink and fray. The memory of your comments will not.

# Why the Wild Cards Win

Eli Manning (#10) and the New York Giants win the 2008 Super Bowl

**April 2008** – Two of the last three Super Bowls have been won by wild-card teams—the Giants this year and the Pittsburgh Steelers in 2006. Of the last 11 Super Bowls, five had a wild-card team in them. Think about that. A team that could not even win its own division has made it to the Super Bowl almost half of the time! Technically speaking (which of course means Las Vegas odds speaking), no wild-card winner should ever win a championship or even get to the Super Bowl, yet they do. And teams that seem destined to win the championship often don't. In 2005, the Indianapolis Colts started off 13–0. Then they lost two of their last three games and ended up losing to the hot Steelers—a wild-card team—that won it all.

This doesn't just happen in football. Last year, the Dallas Mavericks had one of the best regular-season records in NBA history. But they clinched home-court advantage throughout the playoffs early and then coasted into the postseason, even passing up an opportunity to beat a team—the Golden State Warriors—against whom they matched up poorly. In fact, a victory over the Warriors might have knocked them out of the playoffs. Instead, the Warriors came in as a very hot No. 8 seed and beat the team with the NBA's best record in the first round.

As American sports continue to expand their playoffs, the arithmetic keeps getting crazier. The team with the best regular season-record may not be the favorite to prevail. For three straight years in baseball, 2002 (Angels), 2003 (Marlins) and 2004 (Red Sox), a wild-card team won the World Series. The defending Stanley

Cup champion Anaheim Ducks finished second in their conference last year. The defending NBA champion San Antonio Spurs finished third in their conference.

I have watched this phenomenon over the last five or six years with increasing frustration at teams that don't do everything they can to maintain their winning edge once they have found it. They will clinch their division or conference early and then they will make the inexcusable mistake of throttling down and coasting into the playoffs, ignoring the lessons of recent sports history.

Could you imagine Vince Lombardi saying this to a team before a late-season game: "Men, let's go out there but I don't want to see anyone get hurt. We've got the playoffs to get ready for, so nobody overexert yourself. Let's all conserve our energy for when it really matters." I'm quite certain that I've never seen anything like that on the walls of a CEO.

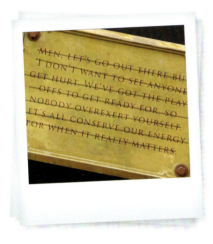

By contrast, I have seen this quote of Lombardi on office walls: "Winning isn't a sometime thing; it's an all the time thing. You don't win once in a while; you don't do things right once in a while; you do them right all the time. Winning is a habit. Unfortunately, so is losing." Lombardi's words explain the recent postseason trend in American sports. The hot team wins. The team that is in the habit of winning continues to win. The team that may have been in the habit of winning but has dialed it down can't get back into the habit of winning.

The "saving yourself for the playoffs" theory no doubt arises from the fear of being second-guessed—the fear that your star quarterback, point guard or pitcher is going to be injured in a late-season game that is meaningless in the standings. You want second-guessing? How about the second-guessing of being the best team in your sport over the course of four or five months and then not winning a championship?

Great teams—championship teams—play their best game every game. There is no meaningless game for them. Did Michael Jordan ever treat a game as meaningless? Great teams and great players don't do the minimum to win; they measure themselves by their own standards, not the standards of others or the standings of their league.

Plus, there is so much that is unknown in sports competition, which is what makes it so intriguing and exciting. You never know which game it will be that will instill confidence in your team or that will cause your team to gel. And you never know what will make it go the other way, either. Thus, teams can ill afford to approach late-season games as meaningless.

There has never been a season that demonstrated this theory more than this last NFL season, and particularly the last game of the regular season. The Giants had been a spotty team throughout the year but had clinched a playoff position, albeit a wild-card spot, before the last game of the regular season against the 15–0 New England Patriots, who had their own incentive not to phone it in because a perfect season was on the line. The Giants played to win, though it meant nothing in the standings, and in so doing received a huge infusion of confidence—Eli Manning in particular. And even though the Giants barely lost that game, that newfound confidence carried over into their first playoff game, which they won. They then beat a Dallas Cowboys team that had the best record in the NFL but seemed disinterested down the stretch, losing two of their last three games. The Giants continued to ride their habit of winning to an improbable Super Bowl victory.

So, coaches and players, beware. "Those who cannot remember the past are condemned to repeat it" (George Santayana, not Vince Lombardi).

# Sharing the Fandom

With Kira and the last two Olympic women's all around gymnastics gold medalists: Nastia Liukin and Carly Patterson

**May 2008** – I've heard the fear expressed by many a new parent—"Well, I guess I'll have to get rid of my season tickets," or "There goes fun as I know it," or similar laments. While it is true from an economic perspective that it's not always easy for a family of four or more to attend a professional game in any sport these days, parents should not be so quick to give up on being spectators. On the contrary, parents should take the wonderful opportunity to view sporting events through a new set of eyes—those of their children. So, given that Mother's Day and Father's Day are fast approaching, I will take this occasion to pay tribute to my favorite sports fan: my 13-year-old daughter, Kira.

Sure, it would have been one option when I began to take her along to sporting events to strap a Walkman (yes, this was pre iPod) on her head and let her listen to the greatest hits of Radio Disney. But I would have denied both her and myself many a wonderful moment. Early in her sports-watching career we devised ways to get her to focus on the game and to get to know the players. For instance, she learned math by doing, as she called it, "hockey math." Example: Wayne Gretzky divided by Mike Modano times Darien Hatcher equals Brett Hull (Hull wore No. 22 when he scored the Stanley Cup game-winning goal for the 1999 Dallas Stars).

At the Winter Olympics in Salt Lake City in 2002, she divided the four flights of skaters in the men's figure skating finals into the "not so good" (those who ranked 19–24 after the preliminary rounds), the "decent" (13–18), the "pretty good" (7–12) and the "very good" (1–6). In one notable moment, the skater who was in approximately 17th place after the preliminary rounds came out for his final routine, the music started, and for the first 20–25 seconds he performed hand movements in the center of the ice without really having taken a stride. "Come on!" she yelled. "Skate!" It is amazing how the voice of a six-year-old could reverberate through a still waiting-to-be-filled Delta Center.

She memorized the flags of the competing countries in Salt Lake City, which set her up well for subsequent school geography tests. She would repeat that feat at later international sporting events (which she describes as a "cool way to bring the world together") that my volunteer positions in sports or legal work allowed us to attend together.

She endured a day atop Alpe d'Huez to watch the Tour de France in 2003 and was on the Champs-Élysées to watch Lance Armstrong win his seventh Tour in 2005. She shot some memorable video footage of the podium ceremony atop my shoulders that day—the soundtrack of our home video being "The Star-Spangled Banner" laced with a 10-year-old voice yelling "Daddy, stand still!"

That same year, she informed me at a baseball game that the triple, not the home run, is the most exciting play in baseball (thus agreeing with Hank Aaron and many others who have come to the same conclusion). Her explanation? "You get to see the guy race around the bases rather than doing that 'pride strut' after he hits a home run."

My daughter has always been able to put things into perspective for me when it comes to attending my favorite sporting events. Last year, we went to see the Texas Rangers play the Chicago Cubs when Sammy Sosa had 599 career home runs. I explained to her that if he hit his 600th home run, he would be only the fifth person in history to accomplish that. Her response? "Oh, well, how many have hit 599?" "The same number," I replied. "Well, then what will be different when he hits 600?" she asked. Hmm. What happened to easy questions like, "Where do babies come from?"

At the Baseball Hall of Fame ceremonies in Cooperstown in 1999, she wore a credential for Nolan Ryan's induction that was as big as her four-year-old frame—exceeded only by the size of the ice-cream cone she worked on as we spent a memorable afternoon at a sidewalk café watching the good and the great in the baseball world drift by us.

I have not always been aware of the full scope of her intake at sporting events. Last year, one Saturday night as she was getting ready for bed, I decided to buy the Floyd Mayweather—Oscar de la Hoya fight on pay-per-view. She asked me what I was about to watch and I told her. "Can I watch it, too?" she asked. I suggested that might not be a good idea. Since it was on pay-per-view, they wouldn't cut to commercials between rounds, and she was likely to hear bad language from the cornermen. "Daddy," she said, "how many sporting events have I been to with you? What word is it that you think I haven't heard?"

Early fandom: Kira at age 1 with Monica Seles

She was given the option of traveling with me to the women's Rugby World Cup in 2006 and the men's Rugby World Cup in 2007, and each time enthusiastically accepted. She was rewarded by being a ball girl at the women's event and by being present for a spectacular score by the U.S. men's team that she described as the "second-most-exciting thing" she'd ever seen in sports, "next to the Stars winning the Stanley Cup."

So fathers (and mothers), don't hesitate to share your interests, your passions and your sports fandom with your children. And may you be as richly rewarded for doing so as I have been.

# Hot Dog Gate

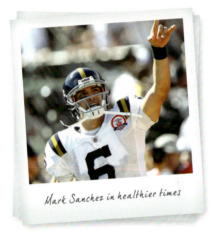

*Mark Sanchez in healthier times*

**December 2009** – Much ado was made about New York Jets quarterback Mark Sanchez eating a hot dog during a television timeout in the Jets' game against the Oakland Raiders on October 25, a game that the Jets won handily. Sanchez wasn't the first player to be seen eating something less than nutritious during an NFL game, nor is he the first athlete to be seen eating a hot dog in uniform. The expansive NFL tackle Nate Newton was once spotted devouring a Snickers bar on the sidelines. And major league pitcher Terry Forster, whom David Letterman referred to as a "fat tub of goo," occasionally had a hot dog in the bullpen during a baseball game. Forster, as self-effacing a guy as there ever was, ended up reveling in his own caricature, even appearing on Letterman's show.

It would be tempting to paint *l'affaire* Sanchez in a cartoonish way and simply let it serve as fodder for late-night TV comedians. However, as President Obama might say, I think there is a "teachable moment" in this episode. In fact, Sanchez's candid and apologetic comments after the game helped to underscore a lesson that I think is one of the most important discoveries a child can make through participation in youth sports.

What Sanchez explained, still in uniform on the field, was that he had been feeling queasy during the week, had a terrible stomachache before the game, couldn't eat much and felt that he needed to get something into his stomach during the game. (As an aside, why there were no energy bars or other more suitable nutrition on the sidelines remains a mystery.) Nevertheless, Sanchez performed admirably in the game even before eating his mustard-laden hot dog.

This was undoubtedly not the first time that Sanchez felt less than 100 percent ready for a game, yet it probably was the first time he had to make a public explanation that revealed his condition. Therein lies the teachable moment. It is tempting to look at pro athletes and see them in world-class condition and not realize that they have to struggle with the same things that everyone else struggles with in day-to-day life—a cold or flu, a sleepless night, a noisy neighbor, emotional upset and the like. Generally, when these things happen in children's lives, they are "excused." If they are sick on the day of the history test, they can make up the test. A note from the doctor or from a concerned mother, and that headache will get them out of PE class.

So how does a child learn that you're not entitled to always feel good when you have to do something of consequence? The answer is through participation in sports. To be sure, other events might allow you a limited time to perform—that school play is happening on only two days, and those might be the two days after you've suffered food poisoning. But no endeavor in a child's life matches sports for consistently teaching the lesson that the event will go on without them, no matter how they are feeling. And so rather than looking for reasons to get out of that event, they learn how to deal with it.

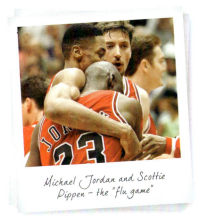

Michael Jordan and Scottie Pippen – the "flu game"

Sanchez helped reveal that those sorts of moments happen more often than we know in pro sports. Athletes overcoming sickness are part of sports mythology. Perhaps the most legendary of "flu games" was Game 5 of the 1997 NBA finals, in which Michael Jordan could barely get out of bed with dehydration, fever and sweating. The series between the Chicago Bulls and the Utah Jazz was tied 2–2, and Jordan rallied from his sickbed to score 38 points and lead the Bulls to a tight victory, before he virtually collapsed into Scottie Pippen's arms. But that was a one-off game that was dramatized to the point of not being translatable to the mere mortal. Sanchez's situation was much more accessible—and as a result it becomes a much more teachable moment.

The sign of a professional is being able to do something well even when you don't feel like it. There is no asterisk by anyone's name when the results of the Masters are published saying: "Would have finished higher if his sinus condition hadn't been aggravated in Augusta." In sports, you learn how to produce your "A" game even though you have a headache or sore throat.

When you've been through enough sporting events where you weren't feeling up to snuff physically or emotionally, but soldiered on and got the job done, that will serve you well on the day of the SAT test when your biorhythms are down. And it will serve you well in adulthood when that presentation you have to make to close a critical sale takes place after a stomach virus has hit in the middle of the night. Thus, rather than stand as the brunt of many jokes, let's let Mark Sanchez and his hot dog symbolize a guy going out and doing a hard job and doing it well on a day when he really didn't feel like it. And unlike with most would-be scandalous behavior in sports, let's hope that the kids were watching.

# In the Trenches

*Kirk Gibson: in the arena*

**November 2010** – One of the great things about watching sporting events when something meaningful is on the line is that it reveals character. Will a basketball player be able to hit the winning shot as time expires in the NBA Finals? Will a quarterback be able to lead his team on a long drive to win a Super Bowl? Will a baseball player be able to hit a walk-off home run in the World Series?

Teddy Roosevelt, the 26th president of the United States, once wrote eloquently about the valor of being "in the arena"— that those who had been in the arena and had their character tested were more to be admired than those who had never been in the fray. The "in the arena" theory certainly holds true today.

But while the limelight may be the ultimate test of character, that character is often built, and may be revealed just as keenly, in the trenches. Therefore it is worth observing how an athlete approaches his or her business outside the limelight. Kirk Gibson is one of those who delivered in the arena, hitting a famously improbable walk-off home run in Game 1 of the 1988 World Series. He absolutely rose to the occasion on a bad leg when the lights were shining brightly.

But I first took notice of him in an early-season game in 1984 when he was with the Detroit Tigers. He sat on the edge of the dugout steps—not in the dugout—when his team was batting. I saw him question an insignificant foul ball call by the third-base umpire, wanting to know how foul it was. When a Tigers player was brushed back and began to make a move toward the mound, I think Gibson was across the third-base line to join the ensuing melee before any of his teammates had left the dugout. He was absolutely the most intense and involved baseball player I'd ever seen. So it was no surprise that year when he led the Tigers to the World Series title. Nor was it a surprise four years later when he resurfaced with the Los Angeles Dodgers and led them to a championship as well. It showed that what goes on in the trenches translates directly to the limelight.

*Walter Payton: in the trenches (Arlington Heights, Illinois)*

Last year, I was at the Visa National Gymnastics Championships. Nastia Liukin, the 2008 Olympic all-around gold medalist, had been heavily promoted for the event, so she was expected to perform in a big way. But she hadn't trained much since Beijing, so she limited herself to just the balance beam competition and put in a rather pedestrian performance. However, what impressed me is that she would even be doing competitive gymnastics a year after reaching the pinnacle of her sport and at a relatively advanced age. Carly Patterson, for example, hung it up at age 16 after cashing in on an Olympic gold medal.

More impressive than Liukin's participation at the 2009 competition, however, is that she showed herself to be a total gym rat. She was at the edge of the mat cheering on her teammates from the WOGA Gym in Texas as well as her Olympic teammates from Beijing. And when I say cheering, I don't mean lightly. Throughout the arena you could hear her encouraging them. She was deeply involved in everything, even helping to prepare the apparatus for her teammates.

Pat Verbeek, the former NHL player known as the "little ball of hate" for his nastiness on the ice, came by it naturally. I saw him in a preseason *practice* for the Dallas Stars late in his career and he got into a fight with a teammate during a scrimmage that left blood on the ice. Perhaps a perverse example of conduct in the trenches, but an example nonetheless.

Walter Payton, for my money the most superbly conditioned athlete of his generation, used to engage in punishing personal workouts, running up and down a hill in a park near his home in suburban Chicago. Athletes of all ages, shapes and sizes would occasionally try to mimic or keep up with him. None ever could. Is it any wonder that he retired as the all-time NFL rushing leader?

So don't just pay attention to star players in their glory. Watch how they approach their craft in less critical moments. More often than not, you will get a preview of how they will perform in the arena.

# CHAPTER 5
# NOT YOUR EVERYDAY PEOPLE

# The Ultimate Survivor

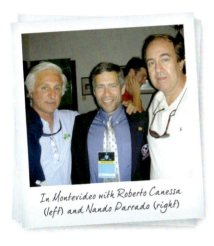

*In Montevideo with Roberto Canessa (left) and Nando Parrado (right)*

**December 2006** – It is the eve of a Rugby World Cup qualifying match between the United States and Uruguay, and I'm enjoying a meal outdoors on a warm, South American spring day at a suburban Montevideo restaurant.

At about this time of year, 34 years earlier, the man with whom I'm sharing food, drink and rugby stories left Montevideo with his rugby team, the Old Christians, bound for a match in Santiago, Chile—a journey that would result in one of the most horrific experiences in the annals of sports-related travel.

He is Nando Parrado. The story of the heroic survival of members of Nando's team after a plane crash 12,000 feet high in the Andes in 1972 has been chronicled in Piers Paul Read's best-selling book *Alive* and Frank Marshall's movie by the same name.

But it is Nando's own book, *Miracle in the Andes* (Crown Publishers), released several months before our visit, which provides the backdrop to our discussion of his survival.

For those unfamiliar with the story, the plane crash killed 16 of the 45 on board, including Nando's mother. Subsequently, 13 more died, including Nando's sister, Susy, either from residual effects of the crash or an avalanche that ripped through the carcass of the fuselage 16 days later.

Sixteen members of the party survived in unfathomable conditions for 72 days nourished (barely) by the liquid they could garnish from snow and (ultimately) the flesh of their departed teammates. And it was Parrado and his teammate, Roberto Canessa, who, after two months at the crash site, walked 70 miles in 10 days, over the highest peaks in the Andes, wearing rag-tag clothes and rugby boots, and led a rescue squad back to their teammates. Indeed the pilot of the helicopter Nando directed back to the crash site continually challenged his directions—believing Nando's trek to be "impossible."

Overcoming injury that left him in a coma for three days after the crash, overcoming freezing cold, starvation, deprivation, personal loss and grief, Nando writes about how he was sustained by the love of, and the "searing need to be with," his father.

Whereas Read's book *Alive* is a stirring documentary, Nando's book is an intensely personal journey about not just how they survived but why.

The Andes crash survivors amongst the wreckage

In an age when we can't be that far away from a Starbucks opening at Everest's base camp, and when the dividing line between billionaires and adventurers becomes blurred, it's important to realize that neither Nando nor any of his teammates sought their status as survivors. He was, in his words, an "untested boy" of 22. Canessa had never even seen snow.

They did not have mountaineering experience, proper clothes, equipment, food or water. But Nando points out that they did have one thing going for them: They were a rugby team. They were used to being in close quarters; they were used to "breathing each other's sweat," relying upon each other and working toward a common goal.

"If we had been a soccer team, we would have died," Nando has said on several occasions and repeats to me on this one. Though what Nando dramatically reinforces in his book is that the ultimate team sport is not one played with a ball or on any confined field. Rather, it is life itself.

Nando fondly remembers the captain of the team, Marcelo Perez, whom he credits with keeping the survivors operating as a team for the first 11 days on the mountain.

"He was a lion on the field," Nando recalls during our conversation. "But can you imagine the pressure on a guy in his early 20s trying to hold things together for an entire group in those conditions?" Perez succumbed to those pressures after his faith was broken upon hearing over the radio on the 11th day that rescue efforts had been called off.

Nando at that point began to assume more of a leadership role in the group, whose numbers tragically diminished five days later when an avalanche claimed Perez and seven others. Rather than be guided completely by his spiritual upbringing, Nando relied on more earthly motivations and experiences: life lessons he learned from his father, his knowledge of and support from his teammates, and the instincts developed from having trained and played a consummate team sport with them.

"The book makes it appear as if there was a lot of planning," says Nando. "And you might think that, because we had 14–15 hours per day to think about things. But I really had to rely on instinct."

Those instincts perhaps best came into play in Nando's choice of Canessa as his partner for the rescue trek. "I needed to choose someone who could push me," Nando explains. Indeed the passage in his book describing his choice of Canessa is not unlike the analysis undertaken by rugby club selectors each week as to who is going to take the pitch on Saturday.

There is one vignette in his book that perhaps reveals both the plight Nando was in and the discipline it took to survive it. A week after the crash, Nando realized he had one piece of food left. This was before the group decision that they would have to overcome a societal taboo—from a society far removed from their own circumstances—in order to survive. The one piece of food in his pocket was a chocolate-covered peanut. So, on that day, Nando sucked the chocolate off of the peanut. The next day he cut the peanut in half and ate one half. The following day he ate the second half of the peanut.

Think about *that* the next time you get back from a dinner party and raid the refrigerator to make yourself a midnight sandwich.

"Your mind starts thinking of ways it can cheat your stomach," Nando says. Then, showing the perspective 34 years can bring, he jokes: "Now I know I could live for three months on a jar of Planters."

What sometimes gets lost in the lore of *Alive* is that Nando is a true rugby man. His heart and soul are in the game, and he has remained connected to and active in the sport to this day—including suiting up for well-situated old boys' events. Roberto Canessa is the current president of the Old Christians club and was proud to have three of his club's players on the pitch for Uruguay against the United States Eagles.

There is a great ease about Nando in person, and he writes with a similar ease. He is not a man who carries the burden of the past with him.

Nando does not view himself as a hero. "I was frightened at all times," he freely admits. He and his teammates were thrust into a situation that could either transform them or finish them. It did the former. "The ability to be truly alive and aware, to savor each moment of life with presence and gratitude, this was the gift the Andes gave us," writes Nando.

It's a gift he shares in *Miracle in the Andes*, a remarkably insightful story about survival, teammates, what parents mean in our lives, and how sport can serve as preparation for life's most challenging moments.

# The Second Time Around

December 2008 – I have often pondered the allure of spectator sporting events involving athletes who have retired from regular pro leagues or tours. I am, of course, distinguishing a senior sporting event from something like a fantasy camp where you interact with your sports heroes in a non-competitive way. I'm referring to paying a hard-earned spectator-sport dollar to go and see players who were once the best in the world but are now well past their prime.

Jim Courier

It's not the same as going to see an aging rock band. Bruce Springsteen just turned 59 but has lost very little speed off his musical fastball. Athletes, however, have a much shorter window of peak performance. Many sports, of course—and particularly team sports—are not conducive to a seniors tour. For instance, a senior boxing circuit—George Foreman's fights of the 1990s aside—would not be a pretty sight. Tennis and golf are the most notable exceptions, each having commercially viable senior events.

I recently had the chance to examine the allure of a senior tennis event by attending a stop on the Outback Champions Series and by enjoying a fortuitous lunch with Jim Courier. Courier, once the No. 1 tennis player in the world, is the founding partner of New York–based Inside Out Sports & Entertainment, which owns and operates the Outback Champions Series. The series consists of eight tournaments for former highly ranked ATP players, with events in Newport, Rhode Island; Naples, Florida; Surprise, Arizona; Boston; Charlotte; Dallas; the Cayman Islands; and Dubai, with hopes for further expansion.

For many tennis fans, the Outback Champions Series provides a "signpost," says Courier. "It takes you back to a time when you and the players were both younger, and looking at them helps you assess how you are now compared to them." In other words, if John McEnroe can still get around a tennis court, I'm not so old after all.

Courier is quick to point out that the Outback Champions Series is "not a victory lap." There is $150,000 in prize money at each stop and a $100,000 grand prize for the player who compiles the most points during the eight series events. Thus, players play to win. While acknowledging that the tour is designed to allow fans to "extend their relationship" with tennis legends, Courier emphasizes that the brand would not have much value if the tennis were not competitive. And as if to prove the point, McEnroe was disqualified from the Outback Champions event in Newport this year for a familiar staple in his repertoire: code violations. McEnroe was thus able to prove Courier's point about the players playing to win and about fans getting a chance to "extend their relationship" with McEnroe (and others), while at the same time proving a recurring point of Dr. Phil: If the relationship was tumultuous the first time around, it will be the second time as well.

From a player's perspective, Courier points out that the players are at the stages in their lives when they can "have their cake and eat it too." They can play highly competitive matches against competitors who are still fit but do so in a collaborative and congenial way, and in a way that reaches out to fans.

Consequently, there is a degree of relaxation to the event. Players will communicate with each other occasionally, and with the crowd, allowing their personalities to come out. For instance, in a match that I saw Courier play against Karel Novacek, he hit a sharply angled cross-court passing shot. Novacek quipped: "You were supposed to go down the line." Courier retorted: "I couldn't follow directions well even in high school. That's why I had to become a tennis player." But despite the entertaining repartee from time to time, most of the unwritten codes of the pro tour are still followed: The players don't speak or make eye contact on changeovers and don't intentionally distract their opponent. The tennis is serious. You may not see the sustained power or frenetic pace of the pro tour and the tactics are not as varied, but there is still plenty of skill on display. As Courier says: "We lose our feet as we get older, but we don't lose our hands."

While several other Grand Slam champions have appeared on the tour—McEnroe, Pete Sampras and, soon, Boris Becker—the goodwill, energy and talent of Courier himself are the driving forces behind the tour. Courier is at different times a promoter, showman, recruiter, spokesman and athlete—making him equal parts the P.T. Barnum, Ringmaster Ned, Lamar Hunt and Don Draper of the Outback Champions Series. At the same time, he is still Jim Courier, as he proved at a recent event by beating Thomas Enqvist of Sweden and taking a decisive lead in the series rankings.

*Rafael Nadal may need a different wardrobe when he hits the seniors tour*

Outback has re-upped its sponsorship, and the tour is well worth a look—even at the risk of the revelation that time has been kinder to your tennis contemporary than it has been to you. Fifteen years from now, however, Rafael Nadal and James Blake may need to change clothing lines before their debut on the champions tour lest they disprove that theory.

# A Team of Individuals

2008 US Ryder Cup Team

**January 2009** – The decision to replace Paul Azinger with Corey Pavin as team captain of the U.S. Ryder Cup is a classic case of "It ain't broke but we'll fix it anyway." Nothing against Pavin, who proved his Ryder Cup bona fides as a player in the early 1990s. But Azinger did something that no other U.S. Ryder Cup captain has been able to do in the previous three tries or in eight of the previous 11: win a Ryder Cup. In so doing, Azinger managed to accomplish a deceptively tricky feat: Take a group of athletes who excel in an individual sport and turn them into a team.

The characteristics that drive individual athletes to success in their particular sport may be the same characteristics that prevent them from being effective members of a team. Nevertheless, Azinger, with an injured Tiger Woods being absent, found the recipe that the previous three captains did not, instituting innovations in his approach to the U.S. Ryder Cup team preparation like splitting the 12 U.S. Ryder Cup players into groups of four for practice (and subsequent competition pairings) based on compatibility.

It isn't just golf where this alchemy occasionally has to take place. The Olympic gymnastics competition, for instance, brings together six accomplished athletes from each country to compete as a team.

In 2008, despite being favored in the Beijing Olympics, the American women's team took the silver medal, leaving the 1996 women's team as the only American Olympic gymnastics team to secure gold in a nonboycotted Olympics (the American men won gold in 1984).

I had a chance to observe the 1996 gold-medal team, the "Magnificent Seven" as they came to be known, when they assembled this past year at the U.S. Olympic Committee Hall of Fame inductions in Chicago. And I couldn't help but notice that even 12 years later they are a close-knit group. So I wondered: Did they win the gold medal because they were so close, or did they become so close because they won a gold medal together? I put that question to the captain of the team, Amanda Borden.

"We knew each other very well, and we had great chemistry," Borden said. "Before the Olympics we had been on tour together for one-and-a-half years." Thus, she credits the team's gold medal in Atlanta to that closeness rather than the other way around.

The 1996 U.S. Women's Gymnastics team: the Magnificent Seven

When I asked Borden why Americans often seem to have a difficult time creating a team concept in an individual sport, she offered an explanation. During the 1996 Olympics, her team was "going against China and Russia and Romania—teams that are together all the time and where they teach you a consistent style and consistent competitive approach." By contrast, her U.S. team brought "different personality styles, different competitive styles and different approaches. We were not automatons."

As the team captain in 1996, Borden made sure that she knew what each of her teammates wanted and when they wanted it. "You need to get to know people on your team," she said. "Some people are the same in the gym as they are out; some people are completely different people outside the gym. You need to know who needs to be hugged, who needs to be kissed, and who doesn't want either."

Borden was also quick to point out the pressures that come to bear when competing as a member of a team, and that those pressures may not be the same as when you are competing as an individual.

"I think all of us felt more pressure representing the team," she said. And she noted that that is why you see more mistakes in the Olympic team competition than in the individual competition, a theory that was borne out by the American women's performance during the games in Beijing.

"It takes a unique personality to be able to compete as a member of a team and then as an individual," Borden said. And on the 1996 team, she pointed out, "everyone had a shot at individual accolades in Atlanta"—making the fact that they were able to gel as a team even more impressive.

Borden is grateful that her coach before the 1996 Olympics, Mary Lee Tracy (who also coached her 1996 teammate Jaycie Phelps), taught her athletes not only gymnastics but also "how to be a great leader and how to be a great teammate," something that perhaps is lacking today in the training of athletes in individual sports. Borden is passing on those lessons to her charges at the gymnastic academies that she runs in Tempe and Chandler, Arizona.

What advice does Borden have for future captains of U.S. Ryder Cup, Davis Cup or Olympic gymnastics teams? "Get to know your teammates," she said. "Develop a heart and soul of the team and then focus on it. Be who you are, let your teammates be who they are, and tap into what you know about each other."

Mr. Pavin, meet Ms. Borden.

# Mr. Old School

*Rod Laver (foreground) vs Ken Rosewall, England 1968*

**September 2008** – This month will mark 40 years since the U.S. National Tennis Championships became the U.S. Open. Prior to that time, tennis had been ruled by an amateur code, and indeed the four major tournaments were amateur affairs. That all changed in 1968, and the first professional tournament to be held in the new "open" era of tennis was the British Hard Court Championship in Bournemouth, England.

One of the participants in that first professional tournament is not as well known in tennis circles as he became known in another sport. He is John Peter Rhys Williams of Wales, known to the rugby world simply as JPR.

JPR Williams had won the British Junior Tennis Championship in 1966, becoming Britain's most promising young tennis player as well as one of its most promising young rugby players. He would later beat future top tennis players such as Dick Stockton and Sandy Mayer. But in April 1968, he found himself in the 32-man draw of that first professional tennis tournament with the likes of Rod Laver, Ken Rosewall and Pancho Gonzalez. He lost, however, in the first round to Bob Howe, an Australian who himself had won several Grand Slam doubles titles.

It was just as well. After losing to Howe, JPR drove 130 miles to Bridgend, Wales, to play in a rugby match—with the selectors for the Welsh National Team in attendance (having no idea that the kid with number 15 on his back had played in the first professional tennis tournament earlier in the day).

He distinguished himself in that rugby match at age 19 and was selected to play for the Welsh national team. He would maintain his position at fullback for Wales for the next 12 years. When he left international rugby in 1981, he had become one of the all-time greats.

JPR Williams

Oddly enough, it was tennis's move toward professionalism that drove JPR to rugby in the first place. His father was a doctor who believed that sports should be amateur, and in 1968, rugby existed under a strict amateur code—a code that would not change until 1995. While JPR was deciding whether to pursue tennis or rugby, he embarked on his own medical career. Ultimately, rugby's continuing amateur code, which allowed JPR more latitude in studying medicine, is what steered him away from tennis.

His multidimensional capacity came in handy on the rugby pitch on several occasions. In New Zealand, while he was playing for the British Lions (made up of the best players from England, Ireland, Scotland and Wales), a player on the New Zealand national team was hit and fell to the ground unconscious. As he was turning blue, it was JPR—playing for the opposing team in a rugby international!—who turned him on his side and cleared his airway so that he could breathe until help could arrive. Even more extraordinary was the time JPR split his head open in a match, went to the sideline, stitched it up himself, and returned to the field of play. Can your modern-day sports hero do that?

I had a chance to catch up with JPR, now 59, at the most recent World Rugby Awards banquet in Paris. Interestingly, he feels that if rugby had been professional in 1968, as it is now, he would have stuck with tennis.

He calls himself a "sports romantic," and the combination of being able to play a team sport at the highest level, while studying medicine, was hard to pass up in the late 1960s. His sports romanticism surfaces when he speaks about things that were lost when sports became professional, which, as he noted, caused the focus to shift unduly to money. For example, the devaluation of the Davis Cup competition is especially disappointing to a man who represented his country on the rugby pitch for 13 years. "It used to be a fantastic event, but the players don't get paid enough to play in it to do so regularly."

He has a mixed reaction to the emphasis on power in the modern tennis game, which is somewhat incongruous to hear from a guy who enjoyed physical collisions. "TV doesn't show how hard they are hitting the ball," said JPR. "The rallies are phenomenal. But I don't think there is as much artistry as there used to be."

Does JPR regret not playing in an era when he could be remunerated for his athletic accomplishments at the level of today's athletes? The answer, for a sports romantic, is of course "no." "I was lucky to play when I did," he says. And he speaks with pride about his Welsh teammates. "We have all done well in our lives. And we stay in touch." And indeed, the camaraderie he shares with his teammates provides further explanation for his decision in 1968 to gravitate away from a professional individual sport to an amateur team sport.

So while a number of the 32 men in that first professional tennis tournament 40 years ago went on to fame and fortune in the world of tennis, there was one man in that draw who is comfortable in his role as doctor, teammate, rugby legend, and one of the last of the sports romantics.

# Banking on Beckham

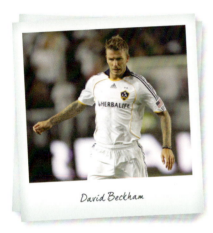

David Beckham

**September 2007** – Well, I was all ready to see it. Billboards in Dallas had advertised it for weeks. Pictures of it were splashed on every newscast. It had even been the subject of a national TV special. I wondered frankly if I would appreciate it when I saw it.

"It" was the much-ballyhooed coming to America of David Beckham. More specifically, it was to be Beckham's first road game with the LA Galaxy—a SuperLiga match against FC Dallas.

Yet, David Beckham was nowhere to be seen when the Galaxy took the pitch. In fact, when the Galaxy boarded the plane for their first road trip in the Beckham era of spreading the soccer gospel, he wasn't there. A turned ankle suffered in one of his last matches with Real Madrid prevented him from playing. Even if he weren't playing, it seemed that his purported role as soccer 's ambassador in the United States would require making the trip with his team instead of hanging back in the Hollywood Hills with his neighbors Tom Cruise and Katie Holmes.

It is perhaps an inevitable result of the risk of promoting one man as the savior of a sport. Just what David Beckham is supposed to "save" American soccer from is unclear. If anything, it is David Beckham who needs to be saved from the numerous local youth soccer players who turned out in Dallas to see the most famous name in contemporary soccer and left without even a glimpse.

The fallout was immediate and instructive. FC Dallas and the Galaxy talked about adding a match somewhere in the schedule so that Beckham's fans in North Texas could see him this year. His next stop in his "Coming to America Tour" was supposed to be Toronto, which he missed as well. Nevertheless, MLS apparently learned its lesson from the disappointment in Dallas and at least had him travel to Toronto. And the promotion of the Toronto match came with enhanced emphasis of the standard policy for sports events that tickets do not come with any guarantee that a player will play the match.

Becks and Posh

The experience in Dallas underscored the confusion of what Beckham's role really is. If he's supposed to be a pop star and bring attention to soccer by getting on the gossip pages, it doesn't matter if he's injured—he should still show up and do whatever a celebrity does. If, however, he is to be an athlete and help his team win, then the promotions by MLS, the Galaxy and road opponents should not be so Beckhamcentric. To truly succeed, the play on the field, and not just that of Beckham, will have to be the sales pitch to sports fans.

Beckham the celebrity began turning into Beckham the athlete several weeks later when he scored off a free kick in the SuperLiga semifinal against DC United and then recorded two assists in the Galaxy's MLS match against the Red Bulls at the Meadowlands. But it is still unclear which role Beckham himself prefers. He will find, though, that Beckham the athlete will be more readily forgiven for an injury, a press conference faux pas, or the antics of a celebrity wife, then will his celebrity alter ego.

And just what is the role of Victoria Beckham—"Posh Spice" to anyone listening to Top 40 radio in the 1990s—in all of this? Since coming to America, Becks has been photographed and been seen more with his wife than on the pitch with his teammates. At this point she appears destined to become the latest Hollywood female celebrity who sits in a prominent seat at sporting events in Los Angeles but whose own career accomplishments are vague—in other words, the role historically filled by Dyan Cannon. What's worse is that in her public appearances Victoria Beckham has been more Surly Spice than Posh Spice. Note to Posh: Your husband is making $50 million a year. Despite a lack of public clamoring for a Spice Girls reunion, your old group is getting back together. Your friend Scary

Spice just mothered a child with Eddie Murphy (who starred in his own version of *Coming to America*). Life is good. It's okay to smile! Instead, you wear the same expression that *I* would have if I found out *my* neighbors were Tom Cruise and Katie Holmes.

It is certainly possible for MLS to use the visibility of Beckham (and Posh too if she can channel Eva Longoria and at least appear to enjoy it) to showcase its sport, as the match at the Meadowlands demonstrated—though it remains to be seen if the true soccer fan will put up with scores of 5–4 (Red Bulls vs. Galaxy) or 6–5 (Galaxy vs. FC Dallas) any more than true baseball fans would continue to turn out to see games that ended 30–3 (Rangers vs. Orioles). But one man does not a team, a league or a sport make. If Beckham draws people to the MLS matches, MLS and its clubs need to be prepared to make fans want to come back, or be happy that they came out, even when there is no Beckham.

MLS does have some things going for it, including underutilized, very modern, fan-friendly new stadiums. Pizza Hut Park in Frisco, Texas, is a magnificent facility. So is Toyota Park in Chicago, and so are others that have been newly built or are in development. They are the type of intimate sports stadiums that the American sports fan hasn't historically experienced.

However, MLS needs to be careful to use Beckham only as a catalyst to encourage people to experience these facilities and the fan experience rather than focusing only on Becks as the greatest show on earth. The true sports fan is a pretty loyal breed; the pop-culture celebrity tracker is not. Whether the Beckham experiment works will depend on his ability to capture the attention of the former rather than the latter.

# LeBron: The Early Years

LeBron James at a September 2009 screening of More Than A Game

**February 2010** – At the 2008 Toronto Film Festival, a little-known movie called *Slumdog Millionaire* won the grand prize. Finishing as runner-up was the documentary *More Than a Game*, directed by Kristopher Belman.

I went to a screening of *More Than a Game* last fall and had a chance to speak with the director. Belman had the good fortune to be from Akron, Ohio, hometown of LeBron James, and to have been a film student at Loyola Marymount at the time the LeBron story was building at St. Vincent–St. Mary High School in Akron. So, needing something to do for his film class, Belman went back to his hometown to capture on film the magic around the high school basketball team.

The film, which will be released on DVD February 2, tells the story of James and his teammates, from fourth grade through their senior year in high school, and it does so in a poignant and effective way. As Belman is quick to point out, the buzz percolating around James in high school was as much about the team as it was about James himself. Belman was determined to make a movie that would reveal the story of the team of friends that stayed together, rather than exploiting his footage of the young James to make it The LeBron Story, which he had many offers to do.

I went to the movie expecting a variation on *Hoop Dreams*, the 1994 film about two inner-city Chicago kids trying to see how far basketball would take them.

As good and as important a movie as *Hoop Dreams* was, *More Than a Game* was richer. Whereas *Hoop Dreams* had a single theme, *More Than a Game* has several: friendship, loyalty, teamwork, David versus Goliath, the coach-player relationship, public school versus private school, and more. Belman's ability to meld these themes makes *More Than a Game* superior to *Shooting Stars*, the autobiography James wrote with Buzz Bissinger that also came out in the fall (win an NBA MVP award and you too can have your life story published at age 24).

LeBron James and high school teammates

The movie obviously creates interest because of James, and not only because of his basketball prowess but also from his personal revelations. As Belman says, a year into his project he had the facts; six years into it, he got the emotion. Thus he was able to capture living-room LeBron, not podium LeBron. But you also get the stories of James's teammates for nine years, Sian Cotton, Dru Joyce III and Willie McGee, plus his teammate for four years, Romeo Travis. In fact, Joyce's father, who coached James and his teammates in junior high school (and later took over as their high school coach), may be the most compelling figure in the film. As the players grow up together, you see them learn lessons about life and sports, including the dangers of arrogance as they lose the state title their junior year. You see them recommit themselves to return to dominance as seniors. You see emotion, as they talk about setbacks they had in eighth grade—an age at which the memory of a missed shot stays with you forever.

Because James and his teammates chose to go to a private high school in order to remain teammates for four more years, the flexibility of the schedule they were able to play was remarkable. They played in UCLA's Pauley Pavilion as high school kids. They played before 10,00 people with Dick Vitale and Bill Walton calling the game. You begin to wonder if they ever went to class. Belman volunteers in conversation that every one of the players graduated with a GPA above 3.4; James had a 3.6.

Belman acknowledges the various themes in his film; he included them so the movie wouldn't be just for basketball fans. It isn't; it works as a human story—a story of growing up and of childhood friendships. But it also works as a basketball movie and includes exhilarating footage of James as a middle-school man-child. It is noteworthy how much of the footage is of the young James making eye-popping passes, not just thunderous dunks.

Belman, a 2004 college graduate, and thus only three years older than the subjects of his film, remains grateful for the access he had to the team. The players affectionately called him Camera Man because he was always around with a camera in the last years of their high school days. Well, Camera Man may be in the process of being upgraded to top-class documentarian.

# The Champ

*Stevie Wonder with Muhammad and Lonnie Ali at the MGM Grand in Las Vegas*

**March 2012** – Muhammad Ali. The words are now so poetic that, in an era when the culture quickly assents to Ron Artest's desire to be called "Metta World Peace," the current generation may not realize how much the former Cassius Clay had to fight—literally and figuratively—to get the world to accept what later became the most famous name in sports. But on the occasion of his 70th birthday party at the MGM Grand Hotel in Las Vegas, in February, an eclectic collection of actors, musicians, boxers and other athletes paid tribute to the man whose outsized legend can be summed up in one word, "Ali," or several alternates: "the Greatest" or "the Champ." In fact, since there are no numbers to retire in boxing, serious consideration should be given to retiring the word "Champ." Thirty-four years after he last held the world heavyweight title and after hundreds of boxers in numerous weight classes have claimed championships, who do you think of when you hear the words "the Champ?"

While in my youth I appreciated Ali as an athlete, there is one moment in my adult life that stands out in revealing what the man meant beyond the boxing ring. On the opening day of the Atlanta Olympics in 1996, I spent the afternoon on a lake in Texas. We docked our boat at a bar along the lake, where the patrons collectively may have had fewer teeth than Leon Spinks, and we settled into place to watch the opening ceremonies. No one knew who would light the Olympic flame, but when Janet Evans ran up the steps and handed the torch to Muhammad Ali, the entire redneck bar broke into a chant of "Ali! Ali! Ali!" Thirty years earlier, such a scenario would have been unfathomable.

Love him, hate him, be turned off by his chosen trade, but Muhammad Ali is the most culturally consequential athlete of the twentieth century. What does it say about the man that so many of his vanquished foes were in attendance to pay tribute to him at the MGM Grand? Norton, Spinks, Foreman, Wepner, Chevalo, Shavers—they were all there. In fact, it seemed as though half the Boxing Hall of Fame was in attendance—Holyfield, Tyson, Leonard, Hearns, Pacquiao, "Boom Boom" Mancini, to name some. Seeing this collection of fighters hearkened back to an era when boxing mattered. It was not only the style and charisma of these great fighters, but also the fact that they seemed to know that they could not exist in their own right. Ali needed Frazier, Leonard needed Hearns, Batman needed the Joker, and they sought out each other to create indelible images from a golden era of boxing, many of which were shown on the MGM's screens. It was interesting that the only current fighter deemed worthy of being included in this pantheon of greats was Manny Pacquiao, a man who, in addition to his record in the ring, seems to share Ali's desire to stand for something more than just boxing, with his service in the Philippines' Congress.

It is hard to imagine anyone who could have brought a wider mix of people together for his 70th birthday party than Ali. There was Steve Schrippa (Bobby Bacala of *The Sopranos*) dining with Joe Perry of Aerosmith. There was Jim Brown seated with Mike Love of the Beach Boys. There were Mike Tyson and Ken Jeong (Leslie Chow in *The Hangover*) to remind us that we were in Vegas. At one point when I pulled out my camera to capture a particular scene, I realized that in one frame I had the unlikely trio of Ali, Snoop Dogg and Buzz Aldrin.

With James Gandolfini at Ali's 70th birthday celebration

Stevie Wonder flew across the country after performing at Whitney Houston's funeral earlier in the day to close the evening's musical entertainment. Lenny Kravitz sang "Black & White America" and John Legend performed "Everyday People," each overtly acknowledging one of the overriding themes of the evening—that a man who started out as a very polarizing figure ultimately earned the respect and admiration of his foes in the ring, of his critics, of the sporting public, and of all races.

And then there was Jerry Jones, who is trying to make Cowboys Stadium a preferred title fight venue, engaged in a live auction bidding war with Ultimate Fighting Championship co-owner Lorenzo Ferttita for the gloves Ali wore in his 1965 fight with Floyd Patterson. The auction ended with words that I had never before heard: "Mr. Jones, you've been outbid." Along with the gloves (which Ferttita acquired for a mere $1.1 million) came a promotional poster for the fight that billed it as "Floyd Patterson vs. Cassius Clay (Muhammad Ali)," with the parenthetical being in smaller font—a reminder of how far the Champ and we have come since 1965.

# CHAPTER 6
# HAPPY TO BE A FAN

# My Olympic Lifeblood

2008 Beijing Olympics – opening ceremony

**October 2008** – I have "predictive text" on my BlackBerry, meaning that (with less than a full keyboard) letters have to share the same key. The "a" and "s" share a key, as do the "o" and "p." So if I stumble when typing "sports," and don't hit the "p/o" key twice, "sports" comes out as "aorta." This BlackBerry-inspired "sports as aorta" metaphor was brought to life during the Beijing Olympics.

I purposely scheduled long-awaited shoulder surgery to coincide with the beginning of the Olympics. If I was going to be immobilized in a recliner, I wanted to make sure I had 24 hours of entertainment. And, like an aorta, the Beijing Olympics pumped entertainment, excitement and inspiration into my otherwise sedentary state.

Thus, my memories of August are not of an uncomfortable recovery, but of the live moments that quickly became iconic images: Michael Phelps exalting as Jason Lezak brought home the gold medal in the men's 4-by-100 freestyle relay, Misty May-Treanor and Kerri Walsh celebrating their second straight gold medal in beach volleyball, U.S. men's volleyball coach Hugh McCutcheon taking a private emotional moment after his Olympic experience went from tragedy to gold medal triumph, and Nastia Liukin and Shawn Johnson posing with gold and silver in the women's all-around gymnastics competition after the most admirable display of competition between friends in a marquee Olympic event since UCLA teammates Rafer Johnson and C.K. Yang in the 1960 Olympic decathlon. Almost equally impressive was the sportsmanship shown by their respective coaches, Valeri

Liukin and Liang Chow—the latter, no doubt, being forever grateful to Johnson that "of all the gym joints in all the towns in all the world, she walks into mine."

Michael Phelps celebrating Jason Lezak's stunning anchor leg in the 4x100 freestyle relay

There were also visible traces of the quaint notion of a U.S. Olympic "team," though a modern-day "team" of 600 is perhaps not as close-knit as the Olympic teams of the early twentieth century that traveled by boat together to Europe. Nevertheless, to see LeBron James and Kobe Bryant cheering for Michael Phelps at the swimming venue was a pleasing modern-day reincarnation of an old concept.

Other world-renowned sports stars also got caught up in the spirit of the Olympics and by their actions showed that it wasn't just another competition. The emotional and unbridled celebration of tennis star Roger Federer, who won a gold medal in men's doubles for Switzerland with his partner, Stanislaw Wawrinka, revealed Federer's reverence for the Olympics. Yao Ming mingled among Olympians from 204 countries at the closing ceremony, not wanting to miss a moment of his country's festival.

Then of course there was the spectacle of the Games themselves, as China staged the most elaborate and expensive debutante ball in history—at least until Bill Gates's daughter turns 18. And the venues themselves, more so than in any Olympic host city in memory, are part of the indelible imagery of the Games that 4.7 billion viewers like me have in their heads. It remains to be seen whether future host cities will now feel compelled to have a feng shui expert as part of their organizing committees.

But the competition consistently surpassed the theater. The incandescent performances of Usain Bolt on the track almost brought me out of my recliner, and probably would have if NBC had broadcast them live. Along with the moments of triumph and joy, there are the inevitable moments of Olympic heartbreak: Dara Torres missing a gold medal at age 41 by 0.01 second, though still showing remarkable grace; the disappointment of 1.3 billion people at Chinese hurdler Liu Xiang's enigmatic withdrawal due to injury. But for me, the ill fate that hit me hardest was that of 100-meter hurdler Lolo Jones, who was comfortably leading the race before hitting the ninth hurdle, stumbling and finishing seventh. Her attitude and candor afterwards made the disappointment even more bitter. Jones, who has a compelling personal background, said within seconds after the race on an NBC interview: "I usually hit a hurdle maybe twice a year. It just sucks that it happened in the most important race of my life." Here's hoping that at age 30 in 2012 Lolo gets a chance to run another important race.

There are of course some unanswered questions, such as: Why did the children's choir in the closing ceremony look older than the Chinese women's gymnastics team? Could the opening and closing ceremonies, with so many characters flying around the stadium, have taken place in a country where there are plaintiff's lawyers? And the question asked by all teenagers and preteens when Jimmy Page played the closing ceremonies: "Who's the old guy looking like he's playing Guitar Hero?"—not realizing they were looking at the prototype for the whole game genre.

Nevertheless, I will always be grateful to the Beijing Olympics for being my "aorta" when I needed it. And I will particularly be grateful to the athletes who every quadrennium prove worthy of our adulation and attention.

# The Sweetest Seven Days

*NCAA Champion Florida Gators*

**July 2007** – The debate has been played out in many a sports bar across the country: What is the best sports week of the year on the American calendar? Before tackling that question, let's get its easy-to-settle twin out of the way: the worst sports week of the year. Actually, it lasts over several weeks: the February lull between the Super Bowl and the beginning of the NCAA basketball tournament. There is a reason *Sports Illustrated* puts out its swimsuit issue around then.

A case might be made that late October is the annual summit of the sports calendar, when the World Series is played, the NFL and college football seasons have taken shape, and the NHL and NBA seasons are just starting. However, if you factor in other popular North American spectator sports, the balance shifts toward the early spring. Occasionally the sports gods serve up such a weeklong buffet for couch potatoes that it leaves no room for debate.

April 1–8, 2007, presented such a convergence. Sports fans were treated to the men's and women's college basketball Final Fours, opening day of Major League Baseball, key NBA matchups, crucial NHL games, a men's and women's golf major, a men's and women's tennis near-major and, for added garnish, a NASCAR race, an IRL race and the World Swimming Championships.

It's not just that men's sports, women's sports, college sports, pro sports, team sports and individual sports were all on display that week. It's that in most cases each of these sports served up the best it had to offer. Consider the men's Final

Four, where Florida successfully defended its national championship against Ohio State. The fact that storied basketball programs UCLA and Georgetown were in the semifinals added to the flavor.

On the women's side, Pat Summitt's Tennessee team reestablished its position atop college basketball with a win over surprising Rutgers (yes, there will be more on this to come).

The opening night of Major League Baseball featured the defending World Series champion St. Louis Cardinals against the New York Mets. April 1 provided a match-up in the NBA between the teams that would finish with the best records in the league, the Dallas Mavericks and the Phoenix Suns, featuring the players who would finish first and second in the MVP balloting, Dirk Nowitzki and Steve Nash.

The NHL was in an all-out fight in both conferences for Stanley Cup playoff position in the last week of the regular season, including a final-game showdown on April 7 between the two most venerable franchises in the league, the Montreal Canadiens and Toronto Maple Leafs, for the last playoff spot in the Eastern Conference (though both would miss out).

Zach Johnson wins the Masters

Men's golf offered its signature event, the Masters, and the drama of up-start Zach Johnson against Tiger Woods looking for his 13th major was compelling. It is a testament to Woods that "the kid," as Johnson was regarded before his breakout moment, is the same age as Woods. Women's golf held one of its majors, the LPGA Kraft Nabisco, won by 18-year-old Morgan Pressel, who became the youngest women's major winner ever. She celebrated by jumping in the pond next to the 18th green with her grandmother, Evelyn Krickstein. Pressel's uncle is former top-10 tennis player Aaron Krickstein, which brings us to the next sport on that week's calendar.

Men's and women's tennis featured the finals of the Sony Ericsson Open. The women's final between a rejuvenated Serena Williams and Justine Henin was spectacular. Guillermo Canas knocked out Roger Federer on the men's side (before losing in the final to Novak Djokovic). The absence of Federer in the first week of April may have been the only blemish in an otherwise perfect complexion of sports greatness for the week, a week that also saw Michael Phelps win his seventh gold medal at the World Swimming Championships.

So what is the legacy of one of the greatest weeks in sports? A week so full of riches would have its place on the mental mantel of every dedicated American sports fan, right? Wrong. What the sports gods giveth, they also taketh away. Plus, this is America, with its unique ability to inject the absurd into an otherwise glorious moment in time. And absurdity, thy name is Don Imus. Absurdity, thy hair is Don Imus. The image we will take away will likely be a goofy talk show host, fired for his inflammatory comments about the Rutgers women's basketball team, or perhaps the critically injured governor of New Jersey, Jon Corzine, who was in an automobile accident on his way to try to sort out the Imus ordeal.

Is there a way to keep the Imuses of the world from screwing up our enjoyment of sports again? Perhaps. Here is what I propose. Let political commentators like Imus, if that is indeed what he is, stick to politics and stay out of sports. In return, sports commentators can (and should) stay out of politics. And if and when another week like April 1–8, 2007, rolls around, it can be remembered for the many top-quality sports events over seven days, rather than for being April fools' week.

# On Frozen Pond

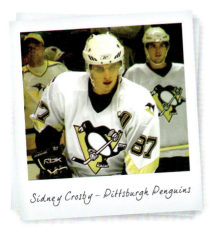

Sidney Crosby – Pittsburgh Penguins

**March 2008** – While leading figures in the NFL and in Major League Baseball are being summoned before Congress over allegations of advanced technical (video spying) and chemical (steroids) wizardry, it almost went unnoticed that another major professional sport in America made a great leap forward by going backwards. I am referring to hockey, and more specifically the first outdoor NHL game ever played on United States soil or ice, when the Pittsburgh Penguins played at Ralph Wilson Stadium in Buffalo against the Buffalo Sabres in what was billed as the "NHL Winter Classic." And it was nothing short of that.

While a capacity crowd at a usual NHL game might be about 18,000 people, more than 71,000 turned out on New Year's Day in the snow to see a game that revealed once again that, despite its best efforts to kill the sport in a players lockout three years ago, the NHL more than any other professional sports league in America can boast players who are truly connected to the essence and roots of their sport.

This game was not some exhibition. It was a regular-season contest between teams in the same conference featuring the greatest talent in the NHL, Sidney Crosby. And even in this unusual setting, Crosby showed why he is the real deal and deserving at age 20 to be the youngest captain in the history of the NHL. Crosby paused during pregame warm-ups to be interviewed on NBC in a fairly substantial snowfall. Just after the opening whistle, Crosby set up the first goal of the game 21 seconds in when he, more than the other players on the ice at the time, realized that the puck would not travel in the snow at the same pace that it would travel in an indoor arena, and picked up a stalled puck to feed Colby Armstrong for the only goal Pittsburgh scored in regulation. Then he scored the winning goal in a shootout. Crosby also brought the broadcast booth to its feet with a midair double puck-juggling move into the Sabres zone that came right off a Canadian pond. And 71,000 people, as well as the largest television audience the NHL has had in many years, were able to see it all.

*Pittsburgh vs Buffalo – 2008 Winter Classic*

It is always refreshing when somebody in American sports gets it right, and the Sabres, the Penguins and the NHL—as well as the league's best player—nailed it with this event. What was most telling is that this game wasn't some gimmick that players begrudgingly participated in to bring publicity to the league on a day— New Year's Day—when football was king. Rather, every single one of the players on both the winning and losing sides, and indeed everyone connected to the event— coaches, broadcasters and the like—would willingly and enthusiastically go back and do it all over again. It was a magnificent spectacle of what hockey is about.

Could you picture the National Basketball Players Association agreeing to play a regular-season game on a concrete court in the Bronx? Could you picture Major League Baseball agreeing to play a regular-season game on a sandlot in Baltimore?

Indeed, the closest MLB comes to its roots is the annual Hall of Fame game in Cooperstown, New York, which is strictly an exhibition game. Even then, in 1999 when the Kansas City Royals played the Texas Rangers, Juan Gonzales refused to take part because his retro-uniform was too baggy and did not show off his physique (even though the game was not being televised!).

Just last month, MLB announced that it would discontinue the Hall of Fame game due to scheduling problems. It is always a delicate balance for a sport to evolve while still keeping its history and traditions intact, but it would have been nice to see MLB go in the other direction and perhaps make the Hall of Fame game a regular-season affair.

Give the NFL credit: There are still games played in historic Lambeau Field in Green Bay, Wisconsin, that take football back to its glory days. Just this year the frozen tundra of Lambeau Field welcomed the NFC championship game and the Packers' playoff victory in the snow over the Seahawks.

The NHL's "Winter Classic" had all the tenacity of a regular-season hockey game while still incorporating some fantasy elements into the event. The playing of the Canadian national anthem and then "God Bless America" before the game, with the players lined up as snow came down on the proceedings, coupled with Irish tenor Ronan Tynan's rather lengthy preamble to "God Bless America," evoked memories of Little Richard doing the pregame honors in the movie *Mystery, Alaska*.

The enthusiasm shown by the players, the showcasing of Sidney Crosby and the television ratings in spite of the fierce college football competition should ensure that we will see this event again. Given that NHL arenas are usually kept at a temperature of 62 degrees, the number of possible outdoor venues for a future game are numerous, and it could be played in warmer climate. There is no reason that it needs to be played in a snowstorm, though for my money that ought to be the case every year.

# The Flat World of Sports

Brian Clay

**May 2009** – There was a time when it was generally thought that the world was flat and the sun revolved around the Earth. Well, astronomers now have a more enlightened perspective, but American network executives are slow to give up the notion that sports viewing revolves around prime-time television—being defined of course as prime time on America's East Coast. So, while Thomas Friedman's popular book *The World Is Flat: A Brief History of the Twenty-First Century* suggests that historical norms and geographical obstacles are being broken down by globalization, the twenty-first century still hasn't completely taken root in American sports programming.

Let's consider NBC's Beijing Olympics coverage. The fact that the rest of the world has a more flexible attitude as to when it can view sporting competitions, coupled with the money NBC plunked down for the TV rights, motivated organizers to place the Games' initial showcase events—swimming and women's gymnastics—in prime time in America, morning in China. This was not ideal, as the women's all-around competition ended at 1:30 a.m. Eastern Daylight Time, not exactly conducive to young, budding gymnasts being caught up by the drama of the live competition.

After the swimming and women's gymnastics had concluded, the decision as to what to broadcast live seemed to be arbitrary. U.S. basketball games were live whenever they occurred, be it 2:30 a.m. or 9:30 a.m. EDT. Most disappointingly, however, the track and field events were almost all on tape delay in America.

Particularly unfortunate was the tape-delayed broadcast of the men's 100- meter final and Usain Bolt's world record performance on a Saturday night in China, even though it could have been shown live at a comfortable time on Saturday morning in the United States—a time when Americans have grown accustomed to watching sports.

The real victim of the decision to broadcast track events on tape delay, however, was Brian Clay, the gold medalist in the decathlon from the USA. Bruce Jenner became a household name after the 1976 Montreal Olympics because his decathlon gold medal drama played out live (of course during prime time in America). Same with Dan O'Brien in Atlanta in 1996. However, the current world's greatest athlete had his signature performance telecast in his home country only via a documentary-style retrospective.

The question to be asked is whether the American sports fan is prepared to watch sports events at what once would have been thought to be peculiar times. We apparently used to think that we could watch baseball only on Saturday afternoon, we could watch football only on Sunday afternoon, and we could watch tennis only on tape delay late on a weekend afternoon. Then, eureka! We realized we could watch football on Monday night. We could watch college football on Thursday night. We could watch Wimbledon and the French Open in tennis, and the British Open in golf, on Saturday and Sunday mornings as they were happening. Later we could watch the soccer World Cup live whenever American teams were playing, even if it was 5 a.m. And Lance Armstrong caused many an American to get up in the mornings and watch the Tour de France on cable.

The first "Breakfast at Wimbledon" on NBC in 1979 was an extremely bold move, but we adjusted. As an aside, the big challenge for that first live broadcast was how to come on the air at 9 a.m. EDT with five minutes of opening montage and remarks, when Wimbledon organizers were adamant that the match itself would start at exactly 2 p.m. London time, 9 a.m. EDT. An elegant solution was reached when Roscoe Tanner, who was playing in the men's final against Bjorn Borg, agreed to stay in the men's room for five minutes, since the match could hardly start without him!

Sadly, that Wimbledon broadcast didn't immediately change the "prime time or not at all" philosophy. Indeed, the Olympic hockey "Miracle on Ice" in 1980 was broadcast live in the Soviet Union at 1 a.m. but not live in the United States even though it was played in the late afternoon.

*Borg vs. Tanner, 1979 Wimbledon final*

Are Americans really that slow in catching up with the rest of the world in this regard—expecting the sporting event to happen when they want to watch it rather than being willing to watch it when it happens, or are sports programmers just too afraid to try to break the mold and find out? It is perhaps instructive that residents of the West Coast seem to be able to adjust to NFL football games being on TV from 10 a.m. to 4 p.m. on Sundays, whereas East Coast residents are comfortable viewing those games from 1 to 7 p.m.

I, for one, like my sports live. It doesn't work for me to pretend that I don't know or can't find out what happened. And I am willing to adjust my schedule to see the broadcast of that live event.

CNN made a bold move several decades ago, banking on the fact that Americans didn't just have to get their news at noon, 6 p.m. and 10 p.m. For those of us who want to see our sports as they happen, and not in repackaged retrospectives, I'm hoping the TV sports world does indeed continue to flatten.

# A Truly Perfect Game

*Mark Buehrle celebrating his perfect game*

**September 2009** – White Sox pitcher Mark Buehrle's perfect game on July 23 in Chicago had a number of noteworthy aspects. First of all, Buehrle became the first pitcher in baseball history to face the minimum 27 batters in a game twice, having thrown a no-hitter in 2007 against the Texas Rangers in which he walked Sammy Sosa but then picked him off base. Additionally, the 27 batters he mowed down on July 23 were part of a string of 45 consecutive batters Buehrle retired (a major league record), taking a perfect game into the sixth inning of his next start on July 28. But what also struck me is that Buehrle's perfect game occurred on an otherwise unremarkable Thursday afternoon in the middle of the baseball season.

We get so used to sports drama playing out before our very eyes with great fanfare that it's unusual for one of the most rare and monumental achievements in American sports to take place somewhat under the radar, at least while it was happening. Generally speaking, anything noteworthy in American sports is covered nationally, and is scrutinized frame by frame as if it were the Zapruder film. If any player is about to do something historic, we are kept up-to-date constantly, with all coverage shifting to the event when it happens. NFL games take place either on weekend days or in prime time when the world can tune in, or at least monitor. In the NBA, if Wilt Chamberlain's 100-point game happened today, word would be out about the time he hit 75 or 80, and we would all tune in to watch it that night. But I would venture to guess that many ardent sports fans, at least those outside Chicago and Tampa Bay (the White Sox's opponent that day), did not hear about Buehrle's perfect game until it was over.

DeWayne Wise saving history for Buehrle

My first reaction was to be somewhat disappointed. For instance, I would love to have been able to share in the drama of DeWayne Wise's spectacular, juggling catch, reaching over the center-field wall in the ninth inning to rob Gabe Kapler of a home run. Would he drop it or not? I would have appreciated the opportunity to look for any hitch in Buehrle's consistent, workmanlike manner as he approached a milestone so rare that only 17 other pitchers in the 134-year history of Major League Baseball had accomplished it (between April 1922 and October 1956, a span of 34 years, there were no perfect games). I would have liked to have been on the edge of my seat as Buehrle faced his 27th batter. You think it's easy to get that 27th out if you've already retired 26? Think again. Nine times a pitcher has retired the first 26 batters he faced only to lose a perfect game facing the 27th. In other words, a full 33 percent of pitchers who have been in a situation where they only needed one more out for a perfect game have not been able to get it done.

Yet, as I came to terms with my own obliviousness to what had unfolded that afternoon while I was going about my own day job, I began to think that there is something a bit refreshing about the fact that even today, when all types of communication methods would alert us to an impending historic event, such an event in our most historic of sports could take place with little contemporary fanfare or suspension of life as we know it. Buehrle's masterpiece was the first perfect game on a weekday afternoon since Don Larsen's in the 1956 World Series, and the first regular-season weekday afternoon perfect game since Addie Joss in 1908. In other words, this was the first perfect game on a workday in the era not only of the Internet but also of cable television, and the first non–World Series perfect game on a workday in the era not only of television but also of radio. Sure, there were ways to follow the game online if you were alerted to what was happening, but the chances of a substantial chunk of the nation being so alerted are reduced on a weekday afternoon.

It's interesting to contemplate what affects our sports consciousness the most: the indelible memory of something you've actually seen that is reinforced by the emotion of the moment, or the mystique of something that you only hear about later. Whichever way you prefer to capture your historic moments, I take some old school pleasure in knowing that such a superb sports performance can still happen before an intimate and dedicated group of fans without going viral— without Buehrle himself tweeting between innings: "only 6 more to go—hope my infielders don't screw up." It hearkens back to a time before SportsCenter, and nationally televised sporting events every night, and even before predominantly night baseball, when players went to work just like the rest of us and we only talked about it at day's end.

In 1951, after Bobby Thomson hit his famous "shot heard round the world" to clinch the National League pennant for the New York Giants, he traveled home alone via public transportation—just like the rest of the day's commuters. That a lunch-bucket guy like Buehrle could, in 2009, get up in the morning, go to work at the same time as the rest of us, discharge his duties perfectly, and be home in time for dinner—interrupted only by a 30-second congratulatory call from a White Sox fan named Barack Obama—may make his pitching gem all the more perfect.

# Peak Performances

Usain Bolt

**November 2009** – More than a year has passed since the Beijing Olympics, which featured the transcendent performances of Michael Phelps and Usain Bolt, among others. Yet until this summer's World Swimming Championships in Rome and the World Track & Field Championships in Berlin, American sports fans had not seen either athlete perform since Beijing. Instead, for a full year after Beijing we were concerned more with Phelps's out-of-the-pool activities while we wondered what Bolt's true potential was in the 100 meters if he ran through to the tape. And the fact that we had to wait a year before we could see them compete at their peak again causes me to sympathize with the stewards of sports like track and swimming, who have to find ways to attract fans in between Olympics and world championships.

The world championships in these sports provided intriguing subplots, specifically the controversy over polyurethane bodysuits in Rome and the gender of South African middle-distance runner Caster Semenya in Berlin. But let's focus on Bolt. In his last six events at the Olympics and the World Championships, Bolt has broken five world records—lowering the 100-meter mark in Berlin to 9.58 seconds, the 200-meter mark to 19.19, and coming close to the world record he set with his Jamaican 4-by-100 relay teammates at the Olympics. Yet anyone who saw Bolt's 9.69 time in Beijing knew that he could go at least one-tenth of a second faster. Why did it take him a year to do so?

*Michael Phelps*

The answer lies in the fact that track athletes, like swimmers, train for peak performances. There are only a limited number of times per season when the athlete gears up to push his or her limits. "You simply can't be at your peak all the time," says Peter Snell, the great New Zealand middle-distance runner who is now an associate professor of internal medicine at the University of Texas Southwestern Medical Center. Pushing the limits of human capability can't be done every week or even every three weeks. Thus, Bolt's records took place in the two showcase events in his sport. So what if Bolt shows up at a track event in the United States—let's say the Penn Relays—and runs the 100 meters. If he ran a 9.92 or even a 9.75, would the crowd go away disappointed? They shouldn't, says Doug Logan, CEO of USA Track & Field. Logan acknowledges that in track and field you have "competition against a legacy" as well as "competition against an opponent." But he doesn't think that fans will go away happy only if a world record is broken. He also points out that team competition can drive fan interest, as can patriotism. And indeed Logan is exploring ways to create interest in a team competition, complete with flag-waving, by bringing back the historical concept of track duel meets but in an international setting, such as a U.S.–Jamaica meet limited to the sprint distances.

No doubt, such a meet would interest fans. Yet when you are dealing with sports like track and swimming where performance can be so objectively measured in times familiar to us all, we know how well an athlete has performed against his or her historical best, and it can't help but affect our assessment of what we have just seen. It is certainly true that athletes in other sports, like Tiger Woods and Roger Federer, gear up for major championships. Yet when Tiger Woods wins the BMW Championships at Cog Hill, it doesn't look that much different from what he might do at Augusta or Pebble Beach. When Roger Federer plays Rafael Nadal in Madrid (and beats him as he did earlier this year) it may not be as epic as a Wimbledon final, but the effort Federer brings to the table looks very much the same as the effort he puts forth in a major. There is no objective measurement to tell the difference.

In track, because the number of peak performances is limited, they are carefully scheduled. In fact, athletes collaborate to avoid each other when they are not at their peak. Thus, we had to wait a year for a race between Tyson Gay of the United States and Bolt—and they didn't disappoint in Berlin with Gay running a remarkable runner-up time of 9.71. By contrast, Federer and Woods don't avoid anybody at any time (including each other, apparently).

Swimming will face some unique challenges in this regard in the years ahead, and we may be able to see how much fan interest is driven by world records—the "competition against a legacy" in Logan's words. If the performance-enhancing suits that were credited with producing so many world records in Rome are banned, it may be years before the majority of world records in swimming are broken. The NFL is considering eliminating or limiting preseason football—in part because fan interest is limited, we aren't seeing those teams at their best. The outcomes of those games don't matter much to anyone. The challenge for track and swimming is to create competitions that matter to the average sports fan even when their athletes are not at their peak. Having been riveted by the competition in these two sports in Beijing, and having had my interest whetted again by the competition in Rome and Berlin, I hope that they can do so.

# The Canadian Crescendo

*Shaun White*

**April 2010** – The Olympics continue to amaze me. Although all sorts of story lines are plotted out before an Olympics begin, they always seem to write their own lasting narratives. At the same time, they have a unique ability to reflect the spirit and the culture of their hosts. The Vancouver Olympics were no exception to either of these precepts.

Canada is a place that takes a while to really know. It does not hit you with the bombast of some countries or the overt richness of some cultures, but after a while you appreciate and embrace the spirit of its people. Similarly, the 2010 Winter Olympics were a tale of two weeks—from humble and tragic beginnings to redemption, joy and inspiration. All the while, though, the Games presented a colorful cast of characters.

The rivalry between Lindsey Vonn and Julia Mancuso provided much fodder for Midwest vs. California/Mary Ann vs. Ginger-themed debates. Shaun White is one of the most remarkable athletes on the planet for his ability to consistently deliver groundbreaking athletic performances while at the same time channeling Jeff Spicoli from *Fast Times at Ridgemont High*. White's interview with Bob Costas after his gold medal performance in the half pipe was particularly noteworthy for its Spicoli influences, as White accepted Costas's invitation to make a plea for a White House visit, turning to the camera to say: "Obama, if you're watching and would like to have me over for some tea or something, I would be most inclined." And speaking of Spicoli, U.S. female half pipe silver medalist Hannah Teter is living proof that Spicoli did end up mating with Jennifer Jason Leigh's character in the movie.

On the ice, the Edward Scissorshands look in male figure skating proved popular this year, while U.S. gold medalist Evan Lysacek put on a clinic of how to stay above the fray when your vanquished rival (in this case Evgeni Plushenko of Russia, aided by Vladamir Putin himself) offers up something less than grace in defeat.

Apolo Anton Ohno and his Korean opponents continue to have a star-crossed relationship, which is unfortunate since Ohno's consistency in such a chaotic sport—and one that is extremely popular in South Korea—is phenomenal. However, at this point Ohno would be about as welcome in South Korea as Simon Cowell would be at an "Up With People" convention.

Canada beats USA in overtime to win men's hockey gold medal

In the "what were they thinking?" department, Russian ice dancers Oksana Domnina and Maxim Shabalian wore clichéd and hackneyed Aboriginal costumes for "folk dancing" night. It was somewhat reminiscent of *Uncle Tom's Cabin* being performed as a Siamese dance in *The King and I*. Their bad judgment may have cost them a higher podium finish.

But the Olympics are not just about the competitors. They are also about the hosts. And the Canadians showed their resiliency. In the first week, the death of Georgian luger Nodar Kumaritashvili, a major malfunction during the torch-lighting ceremony, significant problems with the ice at the speed skating venue, and the first loss by a Canadian hockey team to the USA in the Olympics in 50 years (featuring the best empty net goal I've ever seen, a game clincher by Ryan Kesler of the United States) provided a lot to overcome.

But the spirit of Canada began to shine through, perhaps best personified by Canadian figure skater Joannie Rochette, who either put the whole country on her back or vice versa as she skated courageously two days after the death of her mother. If you had a dry eye after that—which commentator Scott Hamilton certainly did not—check your vital organs. Other members of the Canadian team began to collect gold medals at an impressive rate in the last five days of the Olympics, leading to perhaps the greatest concluding event of any Olympics anytime, anywhere: the USA-Canada gold medal hockey game that went into overtime and made Sidney Crosby the national hero he always seemed destined to be. So often, the big-time player is the one to make the big-time play—which was true on the American side as well with Ryan Miller's brilliant goaltending and Zach Parise's Mike Eruzione-like tying goal in the final seconds of regulation.

The rousing version of "O Canada," one of the world's most user-friendly national anthems, at the end of that game was a fitting punctuation mark on a memorable 16 days that revealed all the human drama and emotion that characterize the Olympics and provided a well-deserved group celebration for a host country that leaves an equally lasting impression.

# Wild, Crazy and Green

The Green Men entertain the crowd

**February 2012** – I have a peculiar appreciation for a particular breed of person who might be viewed as annoying—if you didn't respect the commitments they have made to get to where they are. I speak of the self-described No. 1 fan of a professional sports team. This is not the official mascot but rather the guy who one day shows up at a stadium with a drum or some nutty outfit and out of 60,000 people manages to be the one leading a cheer. And if he does it for long enough, he becomes an institution. I've always wondered how these aspiring icons get past the idiot stage to achieve the status they now enjoy. In fact, how do they even get past security the first time?

For instance, there is John Adams, the Cleveland Indians "drummer" who has been practicing his craft for 38 years. Initially he bought two tickets, one for himself and one for his drum, until after a few decades the Indians provided him with standing tickets. Wild Bill Hagy, of Baltimore Orioles fame, became such a part of the team's scene in the 1970's and 1980's that when Earl Weaver retired as manager (for the first time) in 1982, his on-field swan song was to impersonate Hagy's O-R-I-O-L-E-S chant.

The latest entrants into this legacy are the Vancouver Canucks' "Green Men"—two guys in green spandex who, in a twisted version of a Blue Man Group act, touch the glass in the visitor's penalty box and do handstands around opposing players who are serving their penance. Or at least they did, until the NHL barred them from actually touching the penalty box glass (labeled a distraction) and doing handstands (allegedly a "safety risk").

So, for anyone looking to join this pantheon of immortals (who were honored in the Visa Hall of Fans exhibit at the Pro Football Hall of Fame until the exhibit was discontinued), I offer these tips on how to get there.

Birdman, the Leprechaun and Barrel Man

1. **Start when your team is in the tank.** When Adams began showing up at Cleveland Municipal Stadium with his drum in 1973, the Indians were 71–91. When Crazy Ray began getting traction as a staple of Dallas Cowboys games in 1962, the Cowboys were 5–8–1. A team will be a lot more tolerant of bizarre behavior when it's desperate for fans and enthusiasm. An alternate but more risky strategy is to try to take advantage of the euphoria that surrounds a team on a roll, and see if you can capture lightning in a bottle—or a barrel, if you happen to be in Denver. Barrel Man appeared during the Broncos' magical 1977 season. In this scenario, your wacky character is viewed as emblematic of the broad appeal of a successful team.

2. **Be prepared to be Cal Ripken.** If you are going to be part of the fabric of the experience at a home stadium, you'd better be at every home game. Barrel Man did not miss a Denver Broncos' game for 30 years (1977–2007). The baseball guys face an even greater commitment. Adams, for instance, missed only 34 games in 38 years (less than one per 81-game season).

3. **Reflect your community.** While Bill Hagy personified the beer-bellied Baltimore guy, Fireman Ed with the New York Jets (he of the "J-E-T-S" cheer) is New York through and through and was an actual NYC firefighter. You get better traction with the fans and are more likely to get the blessing of team or stadium management (after a couple of decades) if they view you as representative of the fan base.

4. **Don't try to export your act.** While actual mascots might be given some tolerance by opposing team fans in a hostile stadium, no such slack is cut to the self-proclaimed knucklehead. Just ask Chief Zee with the Washington Redskins, who once tried to take his act to a Redskins game in Philadelphia. The Eagles fans broke his leg.

5.  **Be of your generation.** Crazy Ray and Wild Bill Hagy came on the scene when you could be "crazy" or "wild" simply by selling electronics at prices too low to be believed. The Green Men represent the performance art of our times—to paraphrase Breaker Morant, it's a new goofball for a new century. Plus, their spandex outfits are more conducive to rigid modern-day security measures than a barrel or a drum.

What other Green Men are incubating out there, not yet sure if they want to make such a commitment to their craft or fanhood? I do hope there are some. Much as this species gets mixed reviews, I would hate to see it become extinct, as it does add to the mosaic of a live sporting event.

# CHAPTER 7
# TAKING A LOOK BACK

# Wish I'd Been There

Muhammad Ali vs George Foreman, 1974

**March 2010** – I was recently asked this question: "Out of all the sports events in history, which one do you most wish you had attended?" It's a useful conversation starter, and so I decided to develop a list of possible answers. I have several criteria for my list. While I would love to have seen Milo of Croton wrestle in ancient Greece, or William Tell in an archery competition in the Middle Ages, the debate really only concerns sports events since the advent of photographs and motion pictures. Second, the list should represent a variety of sports. Third, "milestone" games, like Hank Aaron hitting his 715th home run, do not rate on this list. For a sporting event to truly capture your heart and imagination, something unexpected has to happen, and there needs to be more drama than the simple setting of a record that you know is inevitable. With these thoughts in mind, here's my list.

8.  **"The Rumble in the Jungle"**—Zaire, October 30, 1974. With the current disarray of world boxing, it is hard to remember how monumental a Muhammad Ali fight was. The entire world stopped and took notice, especially when he was fighting a legendary opponent. For purposes of this list, it's a close call between the Thrilla in Manila in 1975 or the fight against George Foreman in Zaire in 1974. The Thrilla in Manila was theater of the highest order, and perhaps the greatest heavyweight fight of all time—between "The Greatest" and his most relentless foe, Joe Frazier. But the Rumble in the Jungle against Foreman is where Ali regained his heavyweight title—a unique setting and a result against the odds.

7. **1985 NCAA Men's Basketball Final**—Lexington, Kentucky. Villanova over Georgetown 66–64. An NBA final or an Olympic basketball final does not evoke the emotion of American college basketball, and this was perhaps the greatest upset in a showcase college game. In second place would be North Carolina State over Houston in 1983. And for sheer brilliance it would be Bill Walton's UCLA Bruins beating Memphis State in 1973 with Walton making 21 of 22 shots.

6. **1960 U.S. Open Golf Tournament**—Cherry Hills, Colorado. While there are a number of worthy entries on this list from the world of golf—including Francis Ouimet winning the 1913 U.S. Open, Jack Nicklaus's final round of the Masters in 1986, and Gene Sarazen's double eagle to win the Masters in 1935—the 1960 U.S. Open was the crossroads of golf history with Arnold Palmer, Jack Nicklaus and Ben Hogan all in contention on the final day. Hogan won his first Grand Slam event in 1946, Nicklaus won his last in 1986. That's 40 years worth of Grand Slam winners in contention on the same day. Palmer won on this day in 1960—his only U.S. Open victory.

5. **Big Ten Track Meet**—Ann Arbor, Michigan—May 25, 1935. The sport of track and field is riddled with historic moments. Roger Bannister breaking the four-minute-mile barrier in England in 1954 would have been interesting to watch, but you knew that that was what he was specifically setting out to do. Jesse Owens winning four gold medals in Berlin in 1936, with the political backdrop of those Olympics, would have been an inspiring sight, but it also would have taken place over a number of days. However, there was a better moment to catch track greatness and Owens specifically. And you could have seen it all within a span of 45 minutes at the Big Ten meet in Ann Arbor in 1935. In those 45 minutes, Jesse Owens set three world records and tied another in the 100-yard dash, 220-yard dash, long jump and 220-yard hurdles.

4. **Bears vs. 49ers**—Chicago, December 12, 1965. This was Gale Sayers's rookie season with the Chicago Bears. Bears coach George Halas did not like using rookies, so he didn't even start Sayers until the third game of the season. The football world realized what a remarkable talent it had when, on a muddy field against the San Francisco 49ers, Sayers touched the ball 14 times, and 6 of those times he ended up in the end zone, either by rushing, receiving or punt returning. While there were many legendary football games to choose from, including the 1958 NFL Championship Game at Yankee Stadium, there

is not another moment of such singular brilliance as this one that took place on a day when you might least expect it, and from a rookie running back.

3. **Wimbledon Men's Final**—London, July 6, 2008. Roger Federer vs. Rafael Nadal. Not every great event in sports history needs to have a grainy black-and-white photo or newsreel to characterize it. This one took place before our very eyes. Before this match I always considered the best tennis match of all time to be the 1980 Wimbledon Final between John McEnroe and Bjorn Borg. When McEnroe himself dubs Federer–Nadal the greatest match of all time, and is also near tears while interviewing the participants afterwards, you know it is something special. It was simply tennis at the highest level it has ever been played, and with the long rain delay it was not even clear it would happen on this day. Yes, it was nearly topped by Federer-Roddick a year later, but not quite.

2. **"Miracle on Ice"**—Lake Placid, New York, February 22, 1980. United States vs. Soviet Union. Need I say more? You want the unexpected?

*Did Babe Ruth really point to centerfield before hitting this home run in the 1932 World Series?*

**1. Game 3 of 1932 World Series**—Chicago, October 1, 1932. This is the most legendary and talked-about moment, from the most legendary figure, in America's national pastime. Babe Ruth allegedly pointed to the center field bleachers before hitting a 2–2 pitch from Chicago Cubs pitcher Charlie Root 440 feet in the direction he pointed. What was he yelling to the Cubs dugout and/or to Root? A box seat at the game and you would have stories to tell for the next 70 years. Plus, you would get the benefit of seeing not one but two home runs from Ruth, as well as two home runs from Lou Gehrig.

# When It's Not Just a Game

*Fonzie and his wrecked motorcycle*

**March 2009** – In an episode of the 1970s TV show *Happy Days*, Ralph Malph wrecks Fonzie's motorcycle. Fonzie is smitten with grief. Howard Cunningham tries to console him and suggests that he shouldn't be taking it so hard; after all, "It's just a motorcycle." Fonzie then gives a long litany of what he and his motorcycle have been through together and concludes by saying that it is his motorcycle that made him "the Fonz." He then delivers the memorable line: "Just a motorcycle, Mr. C? And I suppose your mother was just a mother."

Unfortunately, Fonzie's words have been of little use to me over the years when I have placed heightened importance on a sporting event only to have a sports infidel suggest to me that it is "just a game." The fact is, sometimes the sports world does offer up an event that is so much more than "just a game." But it is awfully hard to convince someone of that fact if they have not experienced it themselves. Usually, they tend to be as unmoved as Howard Cunningham was about Fonzie's motorcycle.

I am happy to report, however, that my search for Exhibit A has finally come to an end. For years, I have looked for something tangible that I could hand to someone and say "Here it is," "Read this," or "Look at this," and they would then understand what a sporting event can mean. To be sure, there have been books and even movies depicting sporting events that transcended just the victory or loss on the day, such as *Seabiscuit*, *Cinderella Man* and *Miracle*.

But nowhere has a sporting event been set up and revealed to be of much greater consequence any better than in John Carlin's book *Playing the Enemy: Nelson Mandela and the Game That Made a Nation.* The game is the 1995 Rugby World Cup final in Johannesburg, South Africa, between the host country and New Zealand. South Africa won in overtime.

Carlin's portrayal of what it did to a nation still trying to come to terms with the wounds of apartheid, and Nelson Mandela's role in several decades of events before the match and in the events surrounding the Rugby World Cup itself, gives me all the fodder I need to preach to the sports unconverted.

*President Mandela presenting the William Webb Ellis trophy to Francois Pienaar*

Rugby in South Africa was historically a sport dominated by the minority white population, and in the days of apartheid the black population would actively root for any national team playing against South Africa. In chronicling how the entire nation, black and white, English and Afrikaaner, Zulu and Xhosa, etc., came to support and revel in South Africa's 1995 World Cup victory, Carlin not only reveals the power of sport but also gives keen insight into how Nelson Mandela got to be Nelson Mandela.

Mandela had no background in rugby, but while he was in prison he made it a point to learn as much as he could about the sport. He also learned to speak the Afrikaans language so that he was ultimately able to talk to his captors and adversaries in their native tongue about their favorite sport. "You don't address their brains, you address their hearts," he said. And Mandela understood the power of sport to appeal to hearts and to connect people emotionally and socially in ways that politics never can.

Political discussions by their very nature are divisive, particularly in a place like South Africa where the law intentionally created division. Mandela, with the vision of a prophet and with monumental charisma, used sport to engage his foes, to transcend politics and to unite the country.

One of many remarkable aspects about Mandela is that he prepared himself for a day that might never have come. It was entirely conceivable that he would end his days speaking about rugby in Afrikaans to his jailers, a fact that makes the discipline with which he held to his vision even more astounding. But through a series of political, diplomatic, social and (yes) violent events, all of which Carlin chronicles in *Playing the Enemy*, Mandela was the president of a new South Africa in 1995 when his country hosted the Rugby World Cup, after the dismantling of apartheid ended South Africa's international sports isolation.

Mandela reached out in particular to the captain of the national team, Francois Pienaar—an Afrikaner who historically would have been on the opposite side of the political spectrum from Mandela—as part of his very public campaign for the country to rally around the team. The scene of Mandela presenting Pienaar with the World Cup trophy remains a stunning visual for anyone familiar with South Africa's history.

Carlin's book is being made into a movie, *Invictus*, with Clint Eastwood directing, Morgan Freeman playing Nelson Mandela and Matt Damon playing Francois Pienaar. No word yet on who will play Pienaar's young son, Jean, whose godfather is Mandela himself. Is there any better proof that it wasn't "just a game"?

# A Lasting Legacy

The iconic photo of the 1961 U.S. figure skating team boarding in New York City

**January 2012** – Among the many milestones recognized in 2011, the 50th anniversary of the loss of the entire United States figure skating team in a plane crash near Brussels in February 1961 was one of the most heart-wrenching. And as 2011 came to a close, the U.S. Figure Skating Association made available on DVD the film it commissioned to recognize the occasion, *Rise*, which not only mourns and celebrates the lives of those lost in the crash but also illuminates the legacy the USFSA created to honor them.

One of the challenges that any national governing body of sport faces is connecting one generation to another—crafting a legacy and creating a sort of NGB DNA that can be passed on to future generations. And what *Rise* reinforces is that the DNA of the USFSA may be as strong as that of any national governing body in the business, though we can only hope that no other NGB has a similar catalyst for its legacy.

The USFSA acted with great dispatch and foresight when only eight days after the 1961 crash it established a fund that would support future generations of budding U.S. skaters. The film skillfully weaves between an unfacilitated discussion among some of those skaters—Scott Hamilton, Peggy Fleming, Brian Boitano, Dorothy Hamill and Michelle Kwan—and video and images of those skaters and the 1961 team. The U.S. champions are extraordinarily natural in their comments (Hamilton's eloquence and pathos are particularly noteworthy) and reveal the connection among generations of American skaters, focusing of course on those lost in the crash: Hamill identifying with the haircut of Laurence Owen and welling up while reading a haunting poem that Owen had written; Hamilton identifying with 16-year-old Doug Ramsay; and Boitano relating to the kids of one of the coaches lost in the crash, Danny Ryan. What each of these skaters has is a sense of wanting to pay it forward as much as they themselves look back.

Stone memorial to the victims of the 1961 crash: Berg-Kampenhout, Belgium

The film quite appropriately focuses on the oft-mentioned stories associated with the crash, including the devastating loss of the Owen family—mother and coach Maribel Vinson-Owen and her two daughters, Maribel and Laurence. But there were also some less familiar aspects of the story. For instance, the 1961 U.S. Figure Skating Championships were the first to be nationally televised (ironically, the telecast was sponsored by Rise instant lather). Thus, a nation that was only recently visually introduced to these remarkably talented skaters lost them all several weeks later. The commentator for that 1961 broadcast was Dick Button, which raises the question: Was this guy ever a kid? It seems as if he was born a figure skating commentator. It was also the early days of graphics on sporting events, and the graphic introducing Laurence Owen misspelled her name "Laurance." TV graphics people would soon learn to consult programs before the competition.

One particular vignette in *Rise* highlights the extent to which contemporary U.S. skaters and support workers are so richly connected to USFSA history. Maribel Vinson-Owen was one of the most influential figures and coaches ever in U.S. figure skating, and years after she died in the crash, one of her protégés, Frank Carroll, became the dean of American figure skating coaches.

However, it was not until the 2010 Vancouver Olympics that Carroll coached his first Olympic gold medalist in Evan Lysacek. Lysacek says in *Rise* that when they walked into a room of supporters, he wearing his just-awarded gold medal and Carroll wearing the coach's medal, the ovation for Carroll was even louder than for Lysacek—a testament to the legacy he represented.

I was in Brussels last year, two weeks after the 50th anniversary of the crash. There is a small stone memorial at the site, where the U.S. Embassy, the USFSA and others had recently laid flowers to mark the occasion. The site is agonizingly close to the runway of the Brussels airport, the target destination of the doomed flight. I was familiar enough with the stories to spend some moments there contemplating the tremendous talent that was lost that day, but also thinking about all of the American skaters I have seen in my lifetime who came out of the legacy of the 1961 team. I am very pleased that the USFSA has now made available a fitting and vivid depiction of all that I thought about that day.

# Making the Call

*Do you believe in miracles?*

**August 2007** – In reviewing some of the most memorable moments in sports, it is noteworthy how many times those moments were enhanced by the call of a sportscaster. Name a moment, and for many of them the call and the play have become inseparable—even before YouTube gave us immediate access to these historical sports gems.

The broadcasters who have uttered words that have fused with a particular sports feat have performed a difficult trick. They have had to capture the spontaneity of the moment, share the amazement of everyone watching and frame the moment for history. It's a daunting trifecta, but generally speaking, the best sportscasters of our times have been up to the task.

Could you picture Tiger Woods's remarkable chip-in off the 16th green at the 2005 Masters, pausing on the lip of the cup with the Nike logo showing before going in, without Verne Lundquist's "Oh wow! In your *life* have you seen anything like that?" Could you imagine watching a replay of the end of the 1980 U.S.-Soviet Olympic hockey game without Al Michaels exclaiming, "Do you believe in miracles?"—a phrase so apt that it has been used for movies, books and any reference to the game? Would Bobby Thomson's "shot heard 'round the world" in the 1951 National League playoff game over the Dodgers have had the same reverberation without radio announcer Russ Hodges's unrepentant pennant celebration—"The Giants win the pennant!"—repeated five times? (By contrast, Ernie Harwell's call for television that day was considerably more subdued and therefore long forgotten: "It's gone.")

Each of these instances underscores what seems to be one of the prerequisites for a memorable sports call: It cannot be rehearsed. Neither Lundquist nor Michaels nor Hodges could have possibly anticipated what they would be called upon to describe. Indeed, counterintuitively, the more time an announcer has to think of what he might say for a particular moment, the less memorable the call tends to be. Perhaps this is why there have been few, if any, memorable calls of milestones in baseball.

To prove this, one need look no further than Jack Buck. When the unimaginable happened—a limping Kirk Gibson hitting a walk-off home run for the Dodgers against Oakland in the first game of the 1988 World Series—Buck was up to the occasion: "I don't believe what I just saw!" Same thing when Buck called the surprising Ozzie Smith home run that won Game 5 of the 1985 National League Championship Series: "Go crazy folks! Go crazy!" However, when he had time to think about what to say when Mark McGwire hit his 61st home run in 1998, he was less than his Hall-of-Fame self: "McGwire's Flight 61 headed for planet Maris." What?!

Sometimes a baseball announcer like Buck has tried to do too much with a pending historical achievement, and other times he has done too little. Such was the case with Phil Rizzuto 37 years before McGwire's feat, when Roger Maris hit his 61st home run and passed Babe Ruth. Rizzuto's call? "Holy cow. He did it. 61 home runs."

To be memorable, the announcer's words need not be poetic. Sometimes it is not what is said but rather the way it is said. Johnny Most's excited "Havlicek stole the ball!" when the Celtics won Game 7 of the 1965 Eastern Conference finals preserved the moment for posterity in one gravelly take. When Michael Jordan made one of the most athletic moves ever by a human being—or any other species—driving the lane against the Lakers in the 1991 NBA finals, initially going for a dunk with the right hand then, in gravity-defying fashion, changing the ball to his left hand and laying it up, all without ever touching the ground, Marv Albert spoke for everyone watching: "Oh! A spec-tac-u-lar move by Michael Jordan!" Nothing particularly memorable about the wording, but the delivery was perfect.

When an announcer is describing a scene in a way that enhances our emotional reaction to it, we actually seem to enjoy the fact that he is caught up in the moment like the rest of us. Television broadcaster Chic Anderson captured the thoughts of everyone watching Secretariat win the Triple Crown with his 31-length victory in the Belmont in 1973, as he continued to tick off Secretariat's lead on the best thoroughbreds in the world. "He's moving like a tremendous machine! Secretariat by 12. By 14 lengths on the turn . . . Secretariat is all alone! By 18 lengths . . . An unbelievable, an amazing performance!"

*Ron Turcotte looks back at the field in the 1973 Belmont*

It's not just on game-winning plays that announcers have captured the moment. Rather, some embarrassing moments have also been accompanied by words that have become identified with the gaffe. Lundquist's call of Jackie Smith's drop of Roger Staubach's pass in Super Bowl XIII said it all. "Bless his heart, he's got to be the sickest man in America!"

To be sure, there have been times when announcers didn't enhance the moment, or simply screamed into the microphone: the Christian Laettner shot that beat Kentucky in 1992, the Kordell Stewart Hail Mary to Michael Westbrook that beat Michigan and the Cal–Stanford "play" were accompanied by what can only be described as noise from the booth. But if you surf YouTube for your favorite play, you will find that those examples are the exception, not the rule.

So my congratulations go to a sometimes maligned profession. When sports brilliance—or ignominy—has needed an immediate historian, in most instances sportscasters have filled that role well, and our audiovisual sports history is much the better for it.

# Time Passages

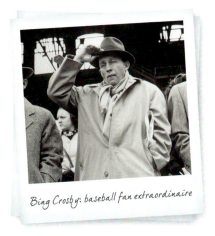

*Bing Crosby: baseball fan extraordinaire*

**January 2011** – The remarkable news that a film had been unearthed of the famous Game 7 of the 1960 World Series between the New York Yankees and Pittsburgh Pirates was cause for celebration for any baseball fan with a sense of history. After all, the game had been hailed as the "best ever," and not just because it ended with the only walk-off home run (by Bill Mazeroski) in a World Series Game 7.

The fact that the film was found in Bing Crosby's wine cellar, however, raised more questions than it answered. Among them: Bing Crosby was a baseball fan and not just a golf enthusiast? Bing owned the Pirates? Home recording equipment actually existed in 1960? Bing actually had "people" to record things on TV that he wanted to preserve, sort of like human DVRs? (OK, the answer to these last two questions is that Bing actually hired a film company to use a kinescope to capture the live television broadcast.)

Of all the questions that this baseball version of Pompeii raises, however, the most significant to me is this: A baseball game of great consequence that ended in a 10–9 score, and included 24 hits and nine pitchers, took only two hours and 36 minutes to play? The length of the game was a testament to a golden era of baseball—indeed there were seven players in the game who had been or were to be named league MVPs. Sadly, there is simply no way that a 10–9 World Series game in modern times could be played in less than four hours, let alone 2:36.

While the temptation would be to blame television for that devolution, that is not where I point the finger. After all, television existed in 1960 as well; otherwise Bing's film company would have had to find other work that day. To have an efficient game, first and foremost, you need pitchers who can get the ball over the plate, and it helps if the starting pitchers have staying power to last late into the game.

*Bill Mazeroski wins it for the Pirates*

I had the pleasure of being at the decisive Game 5 of this last World Series, which featured a terrific pitching duel between Cliff Lee and Tim Lincecum in which each held the other team scoreless for six innings. Lee ended up throwing 95 pitches, 69 of them strikes. Of Lincecum's 101 pitches, 71 were strikes. Both Lee and Lincecum seem to abide by the directives of modern-day pitching coaches: "Babe Ruth is dead. Just throw strikes." Unfortunately for Lee, Edgar Renteria of the Giants is not dead, and he hit Lee's two-out pitch in the seventh inning over the center field fence for a three-run homer that secured the World Series for the Giants.

Lee and Lincecum are rare pitchers who are throwbacks to the Bing Crosby era. Game 5 was played in a speedy 2:32, which allowed kids at the game to get home at a decent hour on a school night and for young East Coast television viewers to watch the whole game. But of course it was a 3–1 game, not 10–9 with a series of relief pitchers, each of them with their own quirks and idiosyncrasies—stepping off the mound before each pitch to rub the baseball, playing with their cap, stepping back onto the mound, deciding they're not quite ready, stepping off the rubber, then finally delivering a pitch. MLB would be well served to cultivate the next generation of fans by limiting the time commitment required to watch a game, and an enforced time clock between pitches would help.

The responsibility for the speed of games does not just rest with pitchers. Batters technically should not be able to step out of the batter's box, adjust their gloves, adjust their pants and comb their hair between every pitch. But there were multiple times in the postseason when Lee, one of the fastest-working pitchers in the game, would be in his windup, the batter would step out of the box and the umpire would call time. If umpires allowed the pitch to continue through the strike zone, batters would stop their slow-down rituals between pitches.

MLB Network's airing of Bing Crosby's tape on December 15 provided a refreshing glimpse of a time when pitchers and batters alike just got on with their business. It is ironic that we have the slow-crooning Bing Crosby to thank for preserving a valuable reference point for the pace at which a professional baseball game is supposed to be played.

# Chasing History

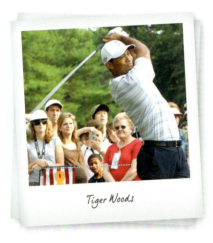

Tiger Woods

**August 2006** – The question of who is the "greatest athlete of all time" is a debate that's familiar to all sports fans. The analysis is not always as complicated as people tend to make it. Two events this summer illustrated this: Tiger Woods's 12th career major victory at the PGA Championship and Roger Federer's eighth career Grand Slam title at Wimbledon.

It is often said that it's difficult to compare athletes from different generations. But one trait that all the "greatest of all time" athletes on my list seem to share is an understanding of history—knowing which measurements of greatness stand the test of time, rather than simply reflecting contemporary standards. Golf equipment, courses and compensation have changed. Tennis equipment, styles and surfaces have changed. But the Grand Slam benchmark has remained constant. Woods and Federer understand that.

Has any athlete ever been more public in chasing the holy grail of his sport—Jack Nicklaus' 18 major championships—than Woods? Perhaps Ted Williams, whose goal was to have people say about him, "There goes the greatest hitter who ever lived." He knew that to be regarded as such he would have to achieve the perfect balance between hitting for average and power. Babe Ruth had a more singular sense of history when he hit his 60th home run in 1927. "Sixty," he said. "Let some other S.O.B. match that."

Professional athletes are motivated by many things—money, fame, next year's contract, which team they play for. There are those who can make a conscious choice between money or a chance for championships. Those who choose the latter are much more inclined to secure their place in history. It may be difficult for an athlete to predict which measure of greatness will ensure his legacy as the generations go by. One who did was Michael Jordan. While he could win an almost unlimited number of season scoring championships (he won 10) it wasn't until he won his sixth team championship, passing Magic Johnson, that he knew he had secured his place as the greatest of all time. If only he had left us with that indelible image of the winning shot against Utah in 1998—sparing us the sight of him in a Wizards uniform—his legacy would have been more intact. For a man with such a sense of history, he succumbed to contemporary temptations. So while we can place him on top of the basketball pedestal, there is something lacking when we compare him with Ted Williams, who homered in his last at bat, or Rocky Marciano, who retired 49–0. The greatest usually seem to know how to go out on top.

Roger Federer

Muhammad Ali, the self-proclaimed "greatest of all time," diminished his legacy by not retiring immediately after the "Thrilla in Manila" in 1975, risking ceding the historical title to Marciano. Ali seemed to be seduced more by the respect he had long sought and been denied—as well as a depleted field of heavyweights after he had vanquished George Foreman and Joe Frazier—and ignored his sense of history. Jim Brown did not make any such mistake. The record for career rushing yards (currently held by Emmitt Smith) will be broken again. But is anyone else likely to lead the NFL in rushing eight of the nine years he is in the league, as Jim Brown did?

Lance Armstrong knew that his sport's Mount Olympus was the Tour de France. He didn't chase Eddie Merckx's records in other cycling events, or even other individual tour records (most yellow jerseys, most stage titles). He went for the top spot in victories, breaking the record with his sixth title and putting it out of reach with his seventh. With this singular focus, did he pass Merckx as the greatest cyclist of all time? Perhaps, but without it he would not be close.

Some athletes have tried to invent a category to declare their historical significance, which tends to relegate an athlete to his or her own time. In 1988, José Canseco confused a statistical achievement with a place in history by declaring himself the first member of the 40/40 club—stealing 40 bases and hitting 40 home runs in a season. This prompted Mickey Mantle to retort, "If I had known it would be such a big deal, I would have done it myself."

Tiger's greatest contemporary rival, Phil Mickelson, does not play with the same sense of history. In Federer's sport, a man who is playing his last Grand Slam tournament this month, Andre Agassi, might have put himself into the bar discussion among the greatest tennis players of all time if he'd only realized earlier that the true measure between generations was victories in majors. He even skipped Wimbledon for three years, before it became his first major title in 1992, being motivated instead by his contemporary image.

Having a sense of history in order to be the greatest may not apply to horse racing, of course. Does a horse know that he has to win the Triple Crown to be in the conversation about the greatest ever? Probably not. But for those of us with two legs and the capacity for abstract thought, if you want to be the greatest of all time, you'd better be able to see outside the confines of your own generation.

# Calls to Die For

*The demise of Diodorus*

**October 2011** – Those of you still awaiting delivery of a recent issue of the *Journal for Papyrology and Ancient Epigraphics* may have missed the revelation that the illustrious history of blown calls by referees can now be traced back at least 1,800 years. That's after a historian, as reported by the journal, was able to decipher the tombstone of a Roman gladiator who was killed in a sword battle that many years ago. The drawings on the tombstone depict the demise of the gladiator, named Diodorus, who was under the impression that his opponent had surrendered while lying on the ground. Diodorus spared his fallen opponent's life, only to have the referee allow his opponent to get back up and plunge a sword into Diodorus. It is perhaps the historical equivalent of a boxer thinking he had knocked out his opponent, only to have the referee rule it a slip. Diodorus's fans, friends or family wanted to make sure that the referee was called out for all of posterity, so they depicted the scene on Diodorus' tombstone, along with the inscription "fate and the cunning treachery of the [referee] killed me."

Friends and fans of modern-day athletes looking to take a final poke at the official who so wronged their heroes may want to take note. For instance, fans of Detroit Tigers pitcher Armando Gallaraga may want to commission an artist to depict Gallaraga's foot hitting first base for what would have been the 27th straight out against the Cleveland Indians in 2010 if not for a blown call by umpire Jim Joyce (no, not that James Joyce). The drawing could be accompanied by the inscription

"He led an 'almost perfect' life"—though Gallaraga's magnanimity in the face of Joyce's gaffe may deter his friends from going all Diodorus when Gallaraga dies.

Supporters of boxer Jack Dempsey, who lost a fight to Gene Tunney in 1927 after ring referee Dave Barry's (no, not that Dave Barry) legendary "long count," that allowed Tunney to get off the canvas despite having been down for at least 13 seconds, could put this on Dempsey's headstone: "Can't you keep the clock going for me?"

In the 1986 FIFA World Cup semifinal between Argentina and England, a goal that was banged in by the hand of Diego Maradona was allowed to stand when the referee completely missed the play. Maradona attributed the goal to the "hand of God." Perhaps English goalkeeper Peter Chilton should consider this for his epitaph: "I hope it's not the hand of Maradona that awaits me."

Tony Tarasco was the Baltimore Orioles' right fielder who was all set to catch Derek Jeter's fly ball in the 1996 American League Championship Series when Yankees fan Jeffrey Maier leaned over into the field of play and caught the ball. Umpire Rich Garcia famously, and incorrectly, ruled it a home run. Maybe Tarasco can take one last swipe at Maier and Garcia by depicting the scene on his tombstone, with the accompanying message: "Please don't reach in."

Philadelphia 76ers Head Coach Doug Collins, as a member of the 1972 U.S. Olympic basketball team, was one of the victims of appalling officiating at the end of the United States–Soviet Union Olympic basketball final in Munich in which the Soviet team was given two "do-overs" in the last three seconds of the game—after Collins had put the United States ahead by a point. I'm sure Collins's entire team would be pleased to commission a mural of various officials—some who had no business being there—conferring at the scorer's table with the inscription on Collins's headstone: "Can I please get two more chances?"

Most recently, in July, the Pittsburgh Pirates were tied for first place when they played a 19-inning game against the Atlanta Braves. The Braves won when Julio Lugo was ruled safe at home by umpire Jerry Meals, despite the fact that Pirates catcher Mike McKenny had clearly tagged him well before the plate. The Pirates' season promptly went into the tank. The play at the plate could be depicted on a monument outside PNC Park in Pittsburgh with the simple dedication: "Here lies the Pirates' 2011 season. Thanks, ump."

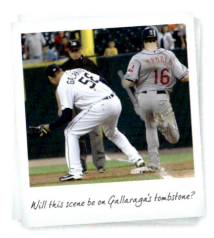

*Will this scene be on Gallaraga's tombstone?*

Each of these gaffes is certainly preserved in our digital archives. But we could make things more interesting for future historians by following in the footsteps of the friends of Diodorus and setting them in stone.

# Speaking of Sports

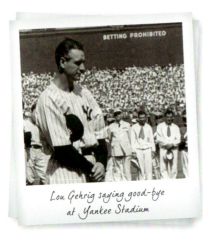

Lou Gehrig saying good-bye at Yankee Stadium

**February 2007** – Among other things that make the presentation of the annual Heisman trophy such a special event is the fact that it is one of the few times when an athlete knows that he is going to have to deliver a speech. Not a statement, not a quote, not a quip in answer to a question, but a speech. It is a lot to ask of a 22-year-old, but on my personal list of "greatest sports speeches," two were delivered by athletes accepting the Heisman Trophy.

To make my list, the speech has to be a true speech, not just a memorable quote. Toward the end of *Bull Durham*, Crash Davis gives Nuke LaLoosh a lesson in all the clichés he will need, such as, "Play 'em one day at a time," or, "Lord willing, things will work out"—thus reinforcing that while athletes may be tutored in the art of the sound bite, speeches are a different matter.

To be sure, there have been some memorable quotes from athletes. Yogi Berra fills up several books' worth. Satchel Paige's philosophy—"Work like you don't need the money, love like you've never been hurt, dance like nobody's watching"—is one of my favorites. But it's a line, not a speech.

Furthermore, the speech must be delivered by an athlete. Bob Costas's eulogy of Mickey Mantle in 1995 was one of the greatest speeches in a sports context ever delivered. But Costas is a broadcaster who gets paid for his words. Similarly, Knute Rockne's "Win one for the Gipper" speech to his team at the 1928 Army game doesn't qualify. Rockne was a coach, not an athlete. Teddy Roosevelt's famous "in the arena" quote is tremendously inspirational, but he was a president.

Of course, there is no rule that great athletes should be great statesmen. But when they have been—particularly when it has come out of nowhere—their words leave an indelible memory. There is one speech that is the pinnacle of sports speeches and is unlikely to ever be supplanted—Lou Gehrig's retirement speech in 1939. As he was dying, he said, "Today, I consider myself the luckiest man on the face of the earth." Sixty-seven years later, watching newsreel footage of that speech still gives you goose bumps.

There is also a clear number two on my list and it came from a man not noted for his speaking prowess at the time, though he has transformed himself into a highly sought-after banquet speaker. When Gale Sayers took the podium in 1970 to accept the George S. Halas Courage Award, no one could have expected that the words he was about to utter, beginning with "I love Brian Piccolo," would be the breakthrough event that would allow men to cry. Try it sometime. Ask any man to admit a time when he cried and more often than not, especially to a casual acquaintance, the first thing out of his mouth will be *Brian's Song*—the movie about Sayers's cancer-stricken teammate about whom he said that night: "Tonight this award is mine; tomorrow it's Brian Piccolo's."

*Nile Kinnick with 1939 Heisman Trophy*

Hall of Fame inductions provide an annual opportunity for memorable speeches. However, so many athletes have become so accustomed to *Bull Durham*-esque clichés that it is hard to turn them off. Nevertheless, Cooperstown provided the setting for the best sports speech I ever saw in person, on July 25, 1999. It also came from an unlikely source—the very private and reserved Robin Yount.

Yount's speech that day was genuine, personal and revealing of his character, and it used sports to make a larger point. Yount's induction came shortly after the death of John F. Kennedy Jr. in an airplane crash. As he neared the end of his speech, Yount said, "We are often reminded how quickly things can be taken from us." Hmm, I thought to myself, Yount has just given a heartwarming tour of all the people who meant something to him in his childhood and career—why would he veer into pop culture now? Yount paused before continuing, "My heart goes out to the families of the men who lost their lives in the construction of the new stadium in Milwaukee." Brilliant! Classic Yount. Blue collar all the way. He concluded, "The game of life can sometimes be too short. So play it with everything you've got." And then he walked off the stage.

As for Heisman Trophy acceptance speeches, there are two that stand supreme above the rest—one famous, one not as famous. The famous is Penn State's John Cappelletti dedicating his 1973 Heisman Trophy to his 11-year-old brother Joey, who was stricken with leukemia. "They say I've shown courage on the football field, but for me it's only on the field and only in the fall. Joey lives with pain all the time. His courage is 'round the clock . . . I want him to have this trophy. It's more his than mine, because he's been such an inspiration to me." Cappelletti's speech later inspired the movie *Something for Joey*.

That speech gets the Heisman for pathos and inspiration. But for eloquence, the modern-day crop of soundbite athletes is unlikely to match Nile Kinnick, the Iowa halfback who on December 6, 1939, concluded his speech in this manner: "Finally, if you'll permit me, I'd like to make a comment, which in my mind is indicative perhaps of the greater significance of football and sports emphasis in general in this country . . . I thank God I was warring on the gridirons of the Midwest and not on the battlefields of Europe. I can speak confidently and positively that the players of this country would much rather struggle and fight to win the Heisman award than the Croix de Guerre." Several years later, Nile Kinnick perished, serving in the military.

The human stories behind the scenes at a sporting event are often what drive our interest in sports. Kinnick's speech, like other great sports speeches, followed that mold, using sports as a backdrop to deliver a genuine human message that stands the test of time.

# Resting at Wrigley

Ronald "Dutch" Reagan

**June 2011** – This is the story of a Cubs fan, and like all stories involving Cubs fans, this one has a bittersweet ending. This particular Cubs fan was born in 1921, thirteen years after the Cubs won their last World Series in 1908, which was, as George Will has so aptly put it, "two years before Tolstoy died." She was born and raised in a small town in Iowa, the second of two children in a family of limited means. Her father was a station agent for the Rock Island Line, and one of the few economic benefits he could pass on to his children was a railroad pass. When the World's Fair was held in Chicago in 1933, he used his railroad benefits to take his family to the biggest city west of New York. And that's when, on a side trip from the World's Fair, she saw it for the first time: Wrigley Field.

The World's Fair was such a success that it reopened in 1934, and she again returned to Wrigley Field, this time as her teenage years were beginning. As the 1930s went on and the Cubs made it to the World Series every three years ('32, '35, '38) she used her father's rail passes to venture into Chicago with her older brother to see the shrine that she would hear described on the radio in Iowa by a local announcer who went by the name of "Dutch" Reagan (later the 40th president of the United States).

These forays from Iowa to Wrigley Field instilled in her not only a lifelong devotion to the Chicago Cubs but also a lifelong knowledge and appreciation of sports. Fueled by the knowledge that dreams could come true and that the imagination could be turned into reality, she managed to put herself through Coe College in

*Wrigley Field*

Cedar Rapids, Iowa, with the benefit of scholarships and by working as the manager of the basketball team. When she graduated in 1942, her version of the *Summer of '42* differed decidedly from the movie. She moved to Chicago to take a position in the accounting department of a major insurance company and, as she described it, she "deliberately" secured an apartment within walking distance of Wrigley Field. In that first summer, she attended every Cubs weekend home game. In 1945, she was there for the Cubs' last World Series appearance—she and her girlfriends having banded together to support a friend who could not afford the $6 admission.

The Cubs' now legendary futility would soon kick in and she found other pursuits, including marriage. Together she and her husband raised three children to whom she passed on her passion for the Cubs and her knowledge of sports.

She taught her children how to keep score at baseball games, and her knowledge of baseball was unrivaled. Indeed, when the coach of her son's Little League baseball team had to be out of town and was searching for a "coach for the day," he didn't look to one of the other fathers or assistant coaches on the team; he selected her. And this was the 1960s.

When one of her children would get upset at a loss in a sporting event she spoke about maintaining an even keel—not getting too impressed with yourself when you win nor too down on yourself when you lose (the latter being critical to a Cubs fan).

When her two sons built an ice rink every year in the backyard, spending hours in the freezing cold and cracking numerous garden hoses, she offered only support—in either verbal or hot cocoa form. When her oldest son played in his first U.S. Tennis Association-sanctioned tournament and drew a highly seeded player in the first round, she was there. But when that opposing player began to deal with the unfamiliar feeling of losing by making questionable line calls, supported by an overbearing mother, she hung back. When her son, in spite of the obstacles faced, won that match, her only words to him were: "I'll bet that felt especially good," thereby teaching her young son that he would have to fight his own battles and that victory includes maintaining your integrity.

She had an innate sense with her children of when to step on the gas and when to put on the brakes; when to go to the whip and when to just let the horses run. When any one of her children was involved in sports she didn't advocate statistics. Instead, she extolled the virtues of "scrappiness"—telling her children that it's a contribution that statistics can't measure but that teammates and coaches would appreciate.

Through all of this, the Cubs were never far from her consciousness. It must have been a very special day for her in 1965 when she first took her children to Wrigley Field to see the Santo–Kessinger–Beckert–Banks–Williams–Jenkins Cubs play the Mays–McCovey-Marichal Giants. And when the Cubs appeared to be breaking out of their futility in that magical summer of 1969, she re-engaged with the resourcefulness she had used 24 years earlier and secured tickets for the first ever National League playoffs—playoffs that everyone thought the Cubs would be in. She didn't reveal to her children that she had done so until Christmas of that year—four months after the Cubs fell out of first place to a surging New York Mets, thereby rendering her tickets worthless. She knew enough about the fate of the Cubs to spare her young children the disappointment of having playoff tickets in hand but no playoffs to attend.

Even that catastrophic season didn't dampen her enthusiasm for the Cubs. Two years later on a family trip to the Northern Ontario wilderness she directed a side trip to Montreal to see the Cubs play the Montreal Expos, then in the third season of their existence. It was poetic validation when the family pulled into Jarry Park in Montreal to pick up tickets at Will Call and Ernie Banks ("Mr. Cub") arrived in a cab for batting practice right behind them, waving and smiling broadly to the Cubs-hat-wearing family. That the side trip to Montreal would be the highlight of this particular family vacation was made clear a week before, at the family "talent" show. The only known fear that she had was of mice and, sure enough, at the rustic cabin where she and her family were staying, one such critter scurried through the kitchen (she calmly summoned her husband who dealt with the situation in medieval style). Strumming a ukulele around the fireplace before the excursion to Montreal, she paid homage to both the late rodent and the Cubs legendary Hall of Fame broadcaster by singing: "I will have to leave my friend the mouse, to see the Cubs and Jack Brickhouse."

In fact, one of the many pursuits she taught to her children was the scrutiny of sportscasters. NBC's pairing of Curt Gowdy and Al DeRogatis in the late 1960s provided particular fodder for her. When Gowdy lauded the potential of a player one time by saying to his broadcast partner, "Yes Al, he's got his future ahead of him," she roared "Ha! There's a revelation. Where else would his future be?!" In one of life's great ironies, her daughter married a sportscaster, albeit one with a thorough command of the English language.

When her children reached an age when they were capable of getting around on their own, she reentered the workforce she had left shortly before the birth of her first child. But this time, rather than jump back into accounting, she took the opportunity to do something she loved and became the assistant recreation director of the village outside Chicago where the family lived.

She and her husband retired to the South in the early days of cable TV, and she was able to spend several decades of retirement watching the Cubs on WGN. She lived a long and exemplary life—a life that recently came to an end in its 90th year. Her last day of consciousness was the day former Cubs first baseman and 1945 National League MVP Phil Cavarretta died. That evening, a barely audible sound came from her bedroom. As her daughter moved closer, the faint sound became recognizable—she was humming the melody of "Take Me Out to the Ballgame."

Before her death, she instructed her children to scatter a portion of her ashes at Wrigley Field, a place where, to her, hope always sprang eternal and a small-town girl from Iowa could actually view the images she only pictured from Dutch Reagan's radio call. Last month, with tears in our eyes and love in our hearts, my sister, my brother and I carried out her wishes.

# ACKNOWLEDGMENTS

The origins of this book are serendipitous. During my service on the U.S. Olympic Committee, I would invariably end up in discussions with Timothy Schneider and Lisa Furfine of Schneider Publishing on the various sports subjects of the day. The discussions would get more robust as last call approached. It was on one of these occasions that Tim suggested that I write a monthly column for Schneider Publishing's magazine, *SportsTravel*. And it was Tim who suggested the title "Winners & Losers," to which I readily agreed, primarily because it was a strong counter to the overused phrase "win-win." There is no "win-win" in sports.

From the spring of 2006 through today, my "Winners & Losers" column has appeared as the last entry in each issue of *SportsTravel*. This has led to several people, including Tim, calling me the poor man's Rick Reilly. They are wrong, of course—I am more like a destitute man's Rick Reilly. Nevertheless, I have been very grateful to Tim and Lisa for the free rein they have given me on the topics I cover.

During my years of writing "Winners & Losers," I have appreciated the work of the editors assigned to make sure that I did not wander too far afield and to make helpful suggestions on the pieces I submitted. Thank you to Lars Thorn, Nathan Price and Jason Gewirtz, the latter having proven himself over many years to be a worthy adversary in any contest of music or sports trivia.

There are two people who were instrumental in encouraging me to turn my monthly rants into a book, and they could not have come from more different walks of life—which suggested to me that maybe it was a viable idea. The first was my mother, Myrna, who after several years of reading my essays asked if I had thought about putting them into a book. But of course, isn't that what mothers are supposed to say? However, when Kevin Roberts, CEO Worldwide of Saatchi & Saatchi, suggested the same thing, the idea began to take root.

Kevin gave me the invaluable introduction to Brian Sweeney of SweeneyVesty. In turn Carla Hofler and Matt Yee at SweeneyVesty helped immeasurably in formatting this book, in securing image permissions, and in countless other ways, including attracting the attention of Greenleaf Book Group LLC. I am indebted to Carla and Matt for their patience and invaluable insight, to Brian for his input, and to Kevin for steering me in their direction.

My appreciation also goes to my assistant of several decades, Cindy Bivins, who would often have to put up with the sound of airplane engines in the background while transcribing my utterances that seemed more often than not to be recorded at 30,000 feet.

But mostly I am indebted to the countless people who made the experiences related in these pages possible, who shared those experiences with me, and who provided insight and perspective on those experiences. Some are named in this book; others are not. But you know who you are.

# INDEX

## A

Aaron, Hank 102, 163
Abdul, Paula 65
Adams, John 158
Agassi, Andre 180
Aguilera, Christina 58
Aikman, Troy 12
Akron Zips 68
Albert, Marv 173
Albert of Monaco 37
Albright, Madeleine 58
Aldrin, Buzz 133
Ali, Muhammad 132, 163, 179
Anaheim Ducks 99
Anderson, Chic 173
Angelou, Maya 68
Annan, Kofi 58
Armstrong, Colby 144
Armstrong, Lance 102, 147, 180
Artest, Ron 79, 132
Azinger, Paul 120

## B

Ballesteros, Seve 52
Baltimore Orioles 128, 158
Banks, Ernie 189
Bannister, Roger 164
Barnum, P.T. 10, 119
Barrett, Michael 95
Barry, Dave 182
Becker, Boris 118
Beckham, David 126
Beckham, Victoria 127
Belichick, Bill 69
Belman, Kristopher 129
Berra, Yogi 9, 90

Bettman, Gary 48
Bieber, Justin 58
Biggio, Craig 95
Bissinger, Buzz 130
Black, Rebecca 58
Blake, James 119
Blatter, Sepp 57
Boitano, Brian 169
Bolt, Usain 138, 147, 152
Bonds, Barry 63
Bono, Sonny 14
Borden, Amanda 121
Borg, Bjorn 147, 165
Bosh, Chris 91
Boston Celtics 69, 173
Boston Red Sox 89, 98
Bowie, David 80
Boy George 74
Boyle, Susan 78
Bradley University Braves 67
Brady, Tom 70, 81
British Lions 124
Brooklyn Dodgers 172
Brown, Jim 133, 180
Bryan, Bob 43
Bryan, Mike 43
Bryant, Kobe 79, 138
Buck, Jack 173
Buehrle, Mark 149
Buffalo Sabres 16, 143
Bündchen, Gisele 53

## C

Caminiti, Ken 95
Campbell, Earl 77
Canas, Guillermo 142
Cannon, Dyan 127

Canseco, José 180
Cappelletti, John 186
Carlin, John 167
Carroll, Frank 170
Carter, Dan 2
Cash, Johnny 67
Cash, Pat 78
Cavarretta, Phil 190
Chamberlain, Wilt 149
Chen, Albert 95
Chicago Bears 39, 164
Chicago Blackhawks 16
Chicago Bulls 69, 78, 105
Chicago Cubs 16, 28, 95, 102,
    165, 187
Chicago White Sox 79
Chilton, Peter 182
Chow, Liang 138
Clay, Brian 147
Clemons, Clarence 59
Cleveland Browns 71
Cleveland Indians 158
Clever, Todd 2
Clooney, George 49
Collins, Doug 182
Connors, Jimmy 85
Cooke, Sam 78
Corzine, Jon 142
Costas, Bob 155, 184
Costner, Kevin 10
Cotton, Sian 130
Coulter, Ann 68
Couric, Katie 68
Courier, Jim 43
Cramer, Richard Ben 61
Crosby, Bing 175
Crosby, Sidney 51, 143

# IMAGE CREDITS